For All I Know
A shebang of checklists for life

This book is for Tom,
the best listener I know.

Contents

Lists Related to Me
(Self-Care)

A Mess

I used to believe life was linear and instead life is a mess.

Every good thing I have has come from either serendipity or a mistake. A big mistake that resulted in a big loss that resulted in something splendid.

As far as I can tell —

There is no why.

Goals are blinders. Serendipity unfolds silently in the outer edges of your noisy hustle.

Be generous. With money, but mostly with your assumptions.

Go create something.

Develop a distaste for lies, even "to protect someone".

Many things you fear are not dangerous.

Learn. Ruthlessly.

Be kind. My every regret stems from giving in to exasperation and impatience.

Many things don't matter. Detect them by asking yourself if they were designed to make you feel more important — or another less important.

Do the best you can. This isn't perfectionism. It's not about the result. It's about effort.

Take care of your people. Be there for them. Let them be there for you. Their way. Not yours.

You can't change or own anyone. You can't "make" anyone anything. Improve them, save them, make them happy.

Love, know and save yourself.

There is so much in connection. If you feel it, run towards it. It's the meaning of life.

Imperatives

Love. Choose love over caution, over fear and over pride.

Love yourself. This is the lens through which you will see everything.

Ferociously go after happiness. It's not something you are — it's something you strive for.

Tell the truth as often and as clearly as possible. A white lie is a lie.

Listen.

Think twice before burning any bridge.

Find silence.

Notice how many mistakes you make that came from you being in a hurry.

Never compare yourself to others.

Create something. You creating something needs you to protect it from every distraction, and in turn it will do the same for you.

How To Be Happier

Live in the present.

Take responsibility.

Identify what you need.

Learn to ask for what you need.

Practice equanimity.

Accept.

Connect.

Assume the best in others.

Grant the benefit of the doubt.

Turn judgment into curiosity.

Keep an open mind.

Be aware. It's where all change begins.

Learn to pause before reacting.

Rest.

Feel the full range of your emotions.

Recognize resistance.

Stand up for yourself.

Stand up for others.

Try new things.

Practice compassion, towards others and towards you.

Set and respect boundaries.

Take nothing personally.

Give.

Be grateful.

Be patient with the things you practice because most are just ideals.

Words for My Younger Self

The single most powerful, most tectonic thing I can tell you is that everything you do every day will add up. Think carefully about what you want to do every day.

There is a world of power and transformation in learning how to pause. Before reacting, pause.

Don't believe everything you think. Question everything, in particular your own thoughts.

Spend no time "being right". The truth is many contradicting things are just as accurate.

Learn as much as you can about boundaries. They are the key to two things you will need forever: healthy relationships and self-love.

You do not need to exert any kind of effort to get someone to love you.

When anyone loves you, how they love you is who they are, not who you are. You will forget this and believe how others love you reveals something about you. It doesn't.

People do not love you the way you want them to. They love you the way they can.

It's normal to outgrow friends.

Fear is not a good decision maker.

Feelings feel like this is the way things will be now, but they are in fact fleeting.

Your life has its own cadence. It does not look like the cadence of another person's life and that's OK. Trust that.

The most important relationship you will ever have is the one you have with you. Stand up for you. Learn to trust you. Love yourself.

A DOZEN GOOD IDEAS TO NURTURE.

To Reduce Self-Esteem

To effectively reduce self-esteem, I need to believe that:

I must be perfect.

Everything I do must be perfect.

Everything I say must be perfect.

Every time I fail it's my fault.

Every time I succeed it's due to circumstances beyond my control.

I am an impostor.

I am not good at anything.

If thinking is good, overthinking is better.

My past is my fate.

I cannot forgive because it implies reconciliation.

Good things happen to other people.

To determine how I am doing I need to compare myself to where others are at.

I have to live up to another's expectations of me.

Disappointing others is not an option.

Ugh. Compliments make me uncomfortable.

What others think of me defines me.

How others behave defines me.

My inner narrative is critical and cruel and she is right.

I have to work tirelessly to get others to like me.

Without this unrelenting effort I am not worth loving.

If I say no to anything I will lose people who are important to me.

One-sided relationships are the best I can get.

I cannot turn my back on relationships that are not good for me, because no one else will love me.

Self-care is selfish.

Life sucks and I have nothing to be grateful for.

4 Habits To Change Your Life

Learn everything you can about setting boundaries, holding boundaries, and respecting the boundaries of others. This habit alone will change the quality of your relationships. The quality of your relationships is the quality of your life.

Tell the truth and follow through on everything you say you are going to do, in particular when you make commitments to yourself. It's a very powerful thing, to teach yourself a bit at a time that you can be trusted. It's how you arrive at believing in yourself.

Pay attention to your inner narrative and every day replace negative thoughts with positive ones. Speak to yourself with the utmost love and respect. You have a loud, relentless warrior inside of you. Imagine what you could do if she was on your side.

Identify what you need and want and get it for yourself. It can be small things like shifting from *"I wish he would bring me flowers!"* to *"I am going to get me flowers!"*, or big things like deciding it's time to be your own priority.

① BOUNDARIES

HERE.

② FOLLOW THROUGH

I WILL.   I DID.

③ POSITIVE THOUGHTS

YEP!

④ IDENTIFY + DECIDE.

THAT ONE.

13

Unexpected Addictions

Worrying, and how worrying begets more worrying without accomplishing anything.

Complaining, and making complaints circular so that action to resolve what I complain about is never taken.

Thinking, and how thoughts pull in more thoughts which pull in more thoughts.

And, being busy. So busy. Feeling guilty about resting or relaxing since our self-worth is tied to how busy we are.

These Beliefs Are All False

There is something somewhere out there I have to somehow find. (A purpose! A soulmate!)

I am the only person in the world who feels anxious, lonely, isolated and insecure and as such I will never tell anyone. (Shhhh.)

If I work hard enough I can make someone love me.

Making someone love me is a good use of my energy.

Failure will destroy me and I cannot afford to make mistakes.

Success means working harder than everyone else.

I need to live up to another person's expectations of me.

Disappointing anyone must be avoided at all costs.

If someone is envious, that's on me.

If someone intimidates me, that's on them.

My worth is measured by my productivity.

Sleep is a waste of time.

Me being critical of myself will somehow result in me changing my behavior.

Changing my mind defines me as wishy washy.

My patterns are my destiny.

I am who I am and cannot alter my personality.

True love does not need boundaries.

Boundaries are a barrier to true intimacy.

Taking responsibility = taking the blame.

Forgiving is forgetting, condoning, excusing — it means a clean slate.

Someone else can make me happy.

If I am not happy all the time there is something wrong with my life.

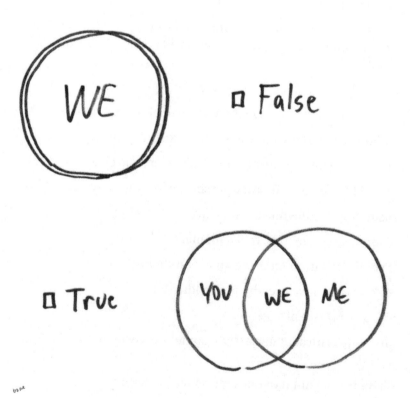

16

How To Keep Promises to Myself

I start really small.

I will take deep breaths for two minutes a day, every day.

I will pick a book that really interests me and read one page a day.

I will go on a 10 minute walk every day.

Then, I can move to bigger promises:

Less blame, more responsibility.

I will learn to say no.

I will pause before reacting.

As I keep my own promises I prove to myself that I can be trusted. I build confidence.

I discover that wherever I go I will always have with me the person I can count on the most.

When Do You Lie to Yourself?

I lie to myself every time I believe I have control over anything.

Every time I think I am finished and have run out of options.

Every time I confuse my perspective with reality.

Every time I believe my memory of things is how they happened.

Every time I tell myself I would do ___, if only I had more time.

Every time I am convinced life will be perfect just as soon as ___.

Every time I fully credit myself for any accomplishment, without attributing anything to circumstance.

Whenever I assume my mistake is an accident and yours is an intent to hurt me.

Whenever I believe I can fix, save or change someone else.

Whenever I confuse something I like with something I know, or something I know with something that's safe.

Whenever I distort information to fit what I already believe.

Whenever I claim things happen for a reason since that's easier to believe than the fact there is no order to the universe, or no one that organizes it for me.

PERCEPTION

REALITY

72DR

Self-Love Today

Today, instead of being hunched up over my computer all day, I will set aside time to stretch.

I will turn things I enjoy — making coffee, taking a shower, winding down to go to bed — into rituals to give them a touch of ceremony and my full presence.

I am going to learn something new just because I think it's interesting, even if I never put it "to good use".

I got myself a book.

I got myself a plant.

I got myself flowers.

Instead of eating lunch at my desk I am going to set the table and take a deliberate break. It will include a cup of tea sipped with zero interruptions.

I will go for a long walk.

Instead of "multitasking" I am giving each thing I do my full attention.

I deserve better than an ambiguous relationship so I'm going to decide *"I don't know"*, *"I am not sure"* and *"maybe"* all mean no.

I will notice how I speak to myself and change any negative self-talk into talk filled with self-compassion.

I will say no.

I will go to bed early.

Picnic by Myself

I bring a big, colorful striped towel and a canvas bag with things I might need: sunscreen, lip gloss, a good book (maybe two), sunglasses.

I bring water and easy, delicious things to eat that don't require a lot of preparation, and a minimal amount of utensils. Finger food!

To be honest with you, I don't get much reading done. Instead, I lie around on the grass watching other people and looking at the sky. In particular I like observing clouds as they go by. I find it very relaxing.

Sometimes pups from neighboring towels come say hello.

If any of this ever makes me feel weird, I do it more rather than less frequently, to give my system a chance to get used to it. Sooner or later I start to crave what once made me self-conscious, and I realize I'm not really by myself. I am with me.

How To Find What I Want

Just because something works for everyone, does not mean it will work for me.

Just because someone loves me doesn't mean they know what's best for me.

Just because I don't know what is best for me does not mean I should just fall back on someone else's idea.

I do not want what "everyone" wants for me.

Just because I'm good at something doesn't mean that's what I should do.

Just because I'm bad at something doesn't mean I can't get good at it.

I don't need more advice. I need less advice. I need time to hear myself.

Contradictions

To me, the better I can hold contradictory statements the better I can make sense of my own emotions.

I feel tired and alive.

I dread and look forward to it.

I am anxious and happy.

I love you and don't.

I love you and don't want to be with you.

I forgive you, and things will never be as they were.

Death is darkness and light.

I both mourn and feel relief. Please no, and thank you.

I love myself. I accept myself exactly as I am. I want to be better.

That thing scares and compels me.

I feel apathetic and hyper-motivated.

I am frustrated at myself and treat me with compassion.

I want and don't want.

I know and I wonder.

I know that's not true and yes, I believe in it.

Life is meaningful and meaningless.

Life is simple and complicated.

Life is beautiful and unfair.

I am learning so much. I know nothing.

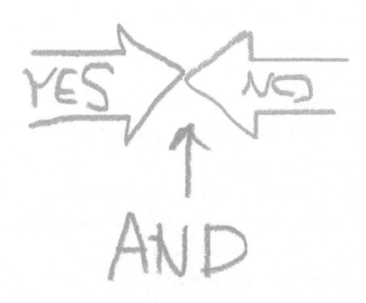

How Do You Know You're Emotionally Exhausted?

I feel trapped.

I feel stuck.

I don't feel like doing anything.

I feel like I can't seem to get enough sleep.

I feel overwhelmed and when I make a list I don't have that much to do.

I feel anxious and cannot pinpoint why.

I feel sad and lonely but instead of searching for company I want to be alone.

I feel angry and easily irritated.

I find noise particularly difficult to tolerate.

I startle easily.

I feel everything is awful, there is no way out and that things will not get better.

I feel jaded and cynical.

Nothing means anything.

Nothing feels good.

I feel disconnected.

I feel zero motivation.

I feel numb.

I feel dread.

I am too tired to set boundaries.

I cannot concentrate.

I keep losing and forgetting things.

I don't know who I am.

I don't know what the point is.

Morning Routine

A morning routine is the antidote to feeling like my day can pounce on me. It's the cure for feeling like my brain is on automatic. It's presence, and it sets the tone for my day.

The truth is it sets the tone for my life but I try to take things a day at a time.

To create a morning routine I start by making a list of things that make me feel centered and nourished. Some examples might be: time (to me, not being in a rush is an enormous, beloved luxury), breath (meditation, or just space to take a few deep breaths), something hot to drink (coffee, chai, even warm water with lemon), something delicious to smell (essential oil), something beautiful to look at (flowers, a beautiful cushion or painting, a cup that feels right in my hand) and something pleasing to touch (a soft blanket, slippers, a plushy robe).

The idea is to salute all my senses, to feel supported and taken care of, looked after by me.

I assemble all these things in a place where I can spend some time with me — a room, a corner, a space.

Then, I make it a habit to go to bed early enough to not mind getting up a bit earlier. Otherwise the temptation that is the snooze button will blow it all.

I set the alarm 30 minutes before I need to get up. (Does this sound like a lot of time? Change it. Even 10 minutes alters my day). When it goes off, I open my eyes, turn the alarm off and pad over to my special place.

Once there, I take a few breaths and decide how I want to spend my time. Sometimes I sip tea and sit alone with my thoughts and my feelings. I also do yoga, stretch. Most of the time, I write.

I love making a list of things I feel grateful for that happened to me on the previous day. I try not to write down anything I have already mentioned on other days so I exercise seeing more things.

If I am not in the mood for any of these things sometimes I just sit by the window and color.

I try to do this every day. If I am not basking in my morning routine I see what I can do to look forward to it, and promise myself to get up early once or twice a week if every day feels like it can't be done.

Finally, I recognize that carving time to spend with myself takes effort and is not always easy so, thank you, Dushka. Thank you for granting me a bit of grace in such perplexing times.

☑ TIME
☑ BREATHE
☑ DRINK
☑ SMELL

Ways To Regulate My Emotions

I am going to sleep on that because early morning helps me put things in perspective.

I am going to take a few days off work because I'm feeling overwhelmed.

I am going to give myself a 10 minute time out to take deep breaths.

Before we sit down to dinner, I'm going to go on a 20 minute walk to clear my head.

I am feeling like I'm biting off more than I can chew. Can we please continue this conversation tomorrow?

Every evening this week I am going to go to bed 40 minutes earlier than I usually do. I am tired and realize I need more than one night to catch up on my sleep.

I am going to learn and practice meditation to take a break from having to think all my thoughts. (I won't stop thinking them but can rest from them.)

I will take all this one step at a time.

Instead of multitasking I will do one thing at a time.

I am going to shorten a couple of meetings to give myself 20 minutes to sit on my couch with a cup of tea so I can catch up with myself.

I need time alone so will not be joining you tonight.

I feel the need for some outside perspective. I am going to go hang out with my friends.

I accept this thing I have been refusing to accept. I realize being at war with reality is unlikely to help me.

Things That Take Courage but Are Not Dangerous

Tell a friend you're in love with how you feel.

Have a difficult conversation. Not via text.

Say no. (In particular if you've been doing something that makes you resentful.)

Say *"enough."* (In particular when you've been feeling taken advantage of.)

Try something new. (Also known as "say yes!")

Speak up — or make room for someone else to.

Stand up for yourself.

Stand up for someone who can't stand up for herself (or himself).

Say you were wrong.

Say you are sorry.

Say you need help.

Walk away from a person or a place that makes you feel stagnant, stuck, or undervalued.

Walk away from a situation that's so comfortable you feel complacent.

Stay in a relationship that's hard but worth it.

Replace blame with responsibility.

Refrain from being defensive.

Resist overexplaining yourself.

Forgive someone who hurt you.

Forgive yourself.

Avoiding My Emotions

If I am avoiding my emotions:

I believe some emotions are friends (happiness! enthusiasm! motivation!) and others are enemies that should be shunned.

I practice a forced, fake positivity which is about pretending to feel what I don't want to feel and rejecting reality. *"I'm fine! Fine, fine, fine!"*

Feeling angry or sad is "bad" and something to run from. This teaches my brain to run from emotions instead of recognizing they are trying to tell me something.

Feeling less than fantastic makes me feel guilt or shame. I mean, other people have it so much worse. What is wrong with me?

I see only what I want to see — my brain creates a filter to block anything that might shatter my artificial, precarious optimism.

I feel anything painful and look for a distraction. Any distraction will do, so I become increasingly less selective about what I'm doing with all my time and energy.

I place all my focus on outside things and none on inside things: my closet is full of things I don't use and my house is full of things I don't need to help me forget that I'm really anxious about my finances.

I keep myself as busy as I can, doing things that don't need to get done. Doing things that don't need to be done contributes to me wondering if this is all there is. This severs me from meaning and purpose.

I never take it easy or slow down lest it all catch up to me which over time makes me feel burned out and always overwhelmed. Of course I am. I am always running.

I postpone any conversation that might feel uncomfortable, difficult or awkward but this need to clear things up or sort them out becomes a weight I carry around. Nothing is ever as heavy as what I need to do but am not doing.

I circumvent any form of confrontation or conflict because it would challenge the notion that things are perfect and that life is like a still photograph of a crystal blue lake.

I try to fix emotions in others. *"No! Don't be sad! Don't you see? Things happen for a reason!"*

I procrastinate on making any decision because my main source of information and a big form of my intelligence are being actively shut down by the fact I don't want to feel.

I blame.

I judge and criticize others, which is really me expressing what I don't like about myself.

I feel disconnected from my life and my body and my friends.

I consume. I eat, I drink, I do drugs, I binge on television, I buy. Yes. More. I become insatiable.

I stop seeing people who try to get me to see what I don't want to see. This sets my filter wrong because I spend less time with people who care.

I avoid being alone, cutting off all contact with the very person I need to talk to the most: myself.

Ways To Calm the Mind

I take long, deep breaths. Inhale to the count of four, hold for the count of four, exhale to the count of eight. This is really hard and feels like I am not doing it right, like it won't work, but it does and it gets easier. One breath at a time.

I talk to myself, replacing my critical inner thoughts with supportive ones. *"It's ok. Everything you are feeling is ok. You are right to feel the way you do. We will work through this, one step at a time. I've got you."*

Move. A run, a walk, a full body stretch, a swim. Moving helps so much. If while I move I take deep, slow breaths, even better.

Change my mental "movie". Instead of living inside my thoughts, I listen to a podcast, watch a movie, read a book. It helps to step outside of my story and into someone else's.

Take a shower or a bath. I add experiences for all my senses. A candle-lit or low-lit bathroom, a delicious smelling soap, good, scrubby gloves.

Write. On a notebook, or on a computer. I write out everything I am feeling. I don't try to write well, or make sense of it, or fix it. I just write.

Do anything creative. For me it's writing but you can sing, paint, dance, draw, make a collage, work on a puzzle. Working on a puzzle is really good for your brain because you show her that things can be put back together, one piece at a time.

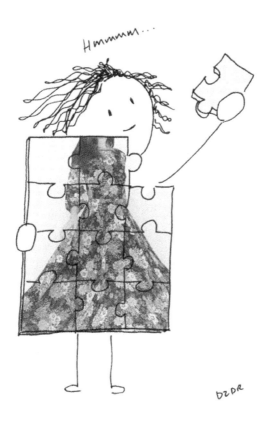

Things Everyone Feels

I don't know what to do with my life.

I don't really know what I want.

I don't really know what I need.

I don't really recognize how I feel.

I don't have it together.

I worry I am not enough.

I look in the mirror and all I see is parts of me I don't like.

I am lonely.

I hide my emotions from others, in particular depression, sadness, anxiety, and isolation.

If I am not distracted, what I feel is despair.

I agree to doing things I don't really want to do.

I fail to stand up for myself.

I have unrealistic expectations so constantly feel I fall short.

I jump to conclusions which means I judge people before I know anything about them.

I regard others with suspicion.

I find it unnatural to celebrate my own victories.

When anyone says *"let go"* I don't know how.

When anyone says *"live in the present"* I don't know how.

When anyone says *"all you need is inside you"* I don't know where.

(I believe feeling all these feelings is inherent to being human, and if we admitted to them we would all feel more "normal", more connected, less alone.)

Preserving My Mental Energy

To preserve my mental energy I try to:

Stop placing myself at the center of everything. The vast majority of things are not about me. This is also known as "not taking things personally".

Stop trying to control what I cannot control, in particular other people.

Stop attempting to "get" or "make" others do anything. This includes any effort to impress another, get someone to like me or approve of me, or making sure others are happy and getting along. It also includes fixing anyone other than me.

Stop trying to meet another person's expectations of me.

Stop managing other people's opinion of me (or of anything).

Stop attempting to get everything perfect.

Stop being led by my ego. She is exhausting.

Stop comparing.

Stop resisting or struggling against how things are. (Or start accepting things as they are.)

Exercise boundaries — saying no is essential to protecting my energy.

Stop overexplaining or justifying. After "no" I don't need to say very much.

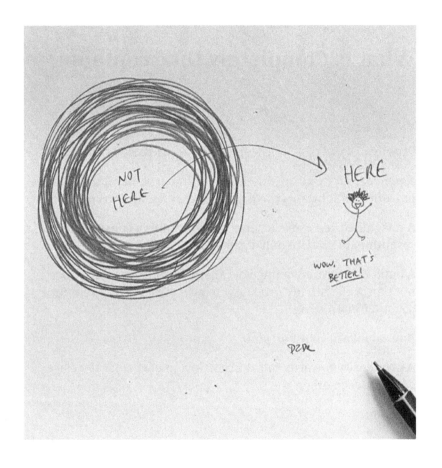

What Is Completely Unacceptable?

Cruelty.

A penchant for putting others down, in particular if the put-down is subtle, as the damage becomes subterranean.

A misguided sense of sacrifice which creates a constellation of resentments that are only visible in the dark.

A habit of taking advantage of others. Maybe because it does not pair well with my proclivity to give myself over to things I consider interesting.

An inability to count on you.

A propensity towards self-destruction, in particular if we are good for each other.

Ketchup.

Self-Trust

You learn to trust yourself just like you would learn how to trust another person:

Spend time with you. Treat this time as you would time with anyone else: talk, listen, connect.

Make small promises to yourself and make sure you keep them, to show you that you can be trusted.

Commit to yourself. This means you don't give up when things go wrong. It means you keep coming back.

Do difficult things first. Difficult tasks, assignments, conversations. To me, procrastination is the opposite of self-trust because putting things off makes for a heavy load you dump on yourself.

Learn something new. It can be simple, like looking up a new word in the dictionary, or elaborate, like learning to cook a cuisine from a far away country.

Feed curiosity. Every time you feel you are judging, making an assumption or putting something down, remind yourself you can hear something new and remain receptive.

Multitasking, overbooking, the sense that you are in a rush, are all self-destructive. Do less.

Before you react, pause. A pause is one of the most valuable gifts you can give yourself.

Cease to accept any relationship that is one-sided. While you're at it, stop believing you have to "earn" love.

Distance yourself from anyone who denies your reality.

Stay away from things that hurt you.

Make your own decisions. It's ok if you start small.

Work out your own problems.

Listen to your inner voice. The more you do, the clearer she will become.

Value your opinion above any other.

Assume responsibility.

Talk to yourself how you'd talk to someone you love. Why would you trust someone who speaks to you unkindly?

Stop comparing yourself to others.

Less control, more surrender. (This is first alarming, then liberating.)

Develop an awareness for sabotaging, undermining, belittling and second-guessing yourself.

Chalk up mistakes as indivisible from life. In fact, chalk up mistakes as indivisible from success. Mistakes: natural, inevitable, indispensable.

Speak up: here is what I think, what I want, what I believe.

Express your boundaries. Say no without remorse, guilt or shame. (I feel remorse, guilt and shame anyway.)

Make sure your significant other is not "your everything". Relationships are a center of gravity for life. But, what about you? What about your interests? What about your friends? What about things you would like to accomplish and that you need time to do? Nurture these things, rather than abandoning them.

Develop an awareness for sabotaging, undermining, belittling and second-guessing yourself.

Treat others in a way that is consistent with all of this — no gossip, judging, putting others down.

Spend a lot of your time creating something.

Feel proud of you.

Assume you are enough, and massively, ponderously worth loving.

What Can We Control?

I can practice having control over:

The things I put my attention on.

The things I put my energy on.

The things I decide to take or not take personally.

The perspective with which I see things.

How I behave.

How I react.

How I communicate.

How I treat others.

My own patterns.

The habits I choose, which add up to a life.

Being fully accountable for all of these things: taking responsibility for what I can control, rather than attempting to control what I cannot, which is anything outside of me.

Why Are We Afraid of Mistakes?

Because what if a mistake defines me?

Because a mistake would imply I am not perfect.

Because if I can't get it perfect it means I am not enough.

Because I don't want to let anyone down.

Because I don't want to be perceived as incompetent.

Because I don't want to be made fun of.

Because a mistake makes me feel ashamed.

Because I don't want to be disappointed in myself.

Because I don't want you to be disappointed in me.

Because I don't want to feel regret.

Because I am afraid.

Because, what if the consequences are incalculable?

Because, what if you won't love me anymore?

Does Your Past Define You?

My past defines me only in that it makes me resilient.

My past, rather than holding me back, grants me experience.

My past is proof that I can both evolve and heal.

My past does not make me unlovable. Instead, it's evidence of my strength.

My past is not something to be ashamed of. It's what makes me both empathetic and compassionate.

My past affects my future only in that it has given me practice in managing change, and in integrating what has happened to me with who I want to be.

I Can't Trust Anyone

When I feel deeply hurt, my thoughts attempt to convince me of many things that are not true, in a misguided effort to protect me.

Here is what they tell me:

I cannot trust anyone.

There is something wrong with me.

I am inadequate.

I am unlovable.

I am broken beyond repair.

The world is a dangerous place and I will never be safe.

All I feel is shame, because I am pathetic.

I am a failure.

Life has no meaning.

I have no purpose.

—

The earlier I get to work on defying these beliefs the better, because every one of them perpetuates itself, like powerful self-fulfilling prophecies.

When I hear my thoughts saying any of these things, I remind them: *"No, thoughts. None of these things are true."*

Too Hard on Yourself

When something goes wrong I often tell myself I should have "trusted my gut".

Or, I should have "sensed" that something wasn't in its place.

Or, that I was not "vigilant" enough.

I should have "picked up on that", been more "perceptive".

I should have "seen" that. I "should have known".

If a friend was describing to me something that went wrong for her, I would never say *"You should have seen that coming."*

I don't expect anyone to somehow know, to do what really comes down to guesswork.

I only expect that of myself.

Being too hard on yourself refers to unreasonable expectations. I will not get everything right. I don't know everything. I do not come equipped with extrasensory perception.

If I find that easy to understand when it comes to others, I should be just as understanding with me.

How To Be an Adult

Develop self-awareness.

Learn about consequences.

Take responsibility.

Learn to love yourself.

Love with your whole heart.

Be careful about the heart of another.

Be a good friend.

Be respectful.

Tell the truth.

Accept feedback with grace.

Learn how to say you are sorry.

Learn to recognize your ego.

Learn to recognize your stories.

Remove yourself from the epicenter of your assumptions.

Develop (good) habits.

Get plenty of sleep.

Eat healthy food.

Learn to cook.

Exercise.

Get a doctor.

Get regular check ups.

Learn basic first aid.

Learn about boundaries.

Respect the boundaries of others.

Vote.

Get a job.

Learn to manage your time.

Take time off.

Keep a to-do list.

Keep a gratitude list.

Keep a calendar.

Show up.

Follow through.

Maintain your email.

Open your mail.

Pay your bills.

Spend less than you make.

Take care of your things.

Be a good communicator.

Spend time alone.

ADULTHOOD

Explaining Myself

I have an urge to explain myself to others.

This urge comes from fear, and from doubting myself. What if you misunderstand me? What if you don't like me? What if you reject me?

I explain myself because if you can't see my side you might think less of me.

If I explain, I might be able to earn your approval. I might be able to make you an ally.

What this tells me is that my impulse comes from wanting to control others and how they perceive me.

But, what if I can just trust myself?

What if your approval or disapproval says nothing about me?

Explaining myself is a huge expenditure of energy. It's pure, fruitless effort, because the bottom line is that I cannot control another person's opinion.

It's me, leaving myself open to being judged or criticized, to second-guessing myself.

Not explaining myself is me, believing in my own choices.

It's me, taking responsibility.

It's me deciding I don't need anyone's permission to do what I believe I should do.

Low Self-Esteem

I am unable to recognize my own worth and can only perceive it through what others say. This creates a self-perpetuating need for external validation.

I avoid conflict, because any form of disagreement threatens my fundamental architecture.

I never set a boundary as I feel that doing so risks my relationships.

I don't respect the boundaries of others because I experience them as a form of rejection.

I am so anxious and wrapped up in how I come across that there is less room for empathy.

I judge others — a symptom that I'm not happy with myself.

I don't trust anyone. Trust is hard to establish with others if I don't trust myself.

I cannot regulate my own emotions.

I cannot communicate my own emotions.

I don't know how to ask for what I want. I am not even sure what that is.

I struggle with two feelings that disguise themselves as coming from others but really come from how I see me: envy and jealousy.

I crave intimacy but am afraid of it.

I want to be vulnerable but it feels too dangerous.

I don't like being alone but also often feel lonely in the company of others.

Low self-esteem is like wearing tinted glasses. It colors everything, because we are the place from where we see the world.

I DON'T LIKE BEING ALONE.

BUT I FEEL LONELY IN THE COMPANY OF OTHERS.

Soothe Yourself

Soothing myself is what I do as a tool to regulate my emotions, my anxiety, anger or stress.

This practice is also useful for winding down and getting a good night of sleep.

When I think of soothing myself it helps me to think of engaging each one of my senses.

Touch. I fiddle with something soft or with a pleasing texture.

Sound. I listen to music.

Sight. I leaf through a beautiful book, or go somewhere where I can see the ocean or a forest if this is available to me.

Taste. I make a cup of stress relief tea.

Smell. I take a bath with good smelling salts. I love essential oils and have a few bottles of them that come with rollers so I can dispense oil on my pulse points (wrists, temples).

Also,

I drink water.

I take slow, deep breaths.

I talk to myself and try to position myself as a witness to what I am feeling.

I place my hands over my chest and feel my heart.

I move: stretch, do yoga, walk, dance.

I color.

I nap or go to bed early.

I write.

What Are Some Beautiful Truths of Life?

You will get your heart broken and unfortunately there is no way around that. But a broken heart will forever impact your ability to see yourself and to understand the pain of others.

Whenever things become too much for you and you need to escape into yourself you will create a world where you make things out of nothing that you can maybe share with others. This will be the safest you will ever feel and if you are lucky your work will lend to another a sense of relief and of wonder.

Others will feel less alone, because of what you make.

You will go through extremely trying times and will learn resilience and adaptation, two of the most liquid, most useful skills in life.

I don't believe in forced positivity or "always looking at the bright side" but I find solace in knowing that it's possible for ugly things to transmogrify into something beautiful.

FROM
TOO MUCH...

CREATE...

SHARE.

Stop Being So Sensitive

What would I need to do, to be less sensitive?

I'd have to harden my heart. Bury my emotions. Dismiss my feelings.

Learn to care less, rather than more.

This sounds like I'd have to turn my back on me, excise precisely what makes me who I am.

Instead, I'd rather be gentle with myself. Assure me there is nothing wrong with me.

Instead of "toughing me up" I'd be careful with what I expose myself to, and be diligent about setting boundaries to protect myself.

Here is what I remind myself of: growth is defined as being more of who I am. More, not less.

I never need to be anything other than who I already am.

More often than not, what I consider a weakness is my strength.

I am not supposed to abandon it. I am supposed to defend it.

Coping Mechanisms

A coping mechanism is anything my fabulously resourceful brain does — often without telling me — to distance herself from something I might find difficult to handle.

How kind of her, how sweetly protective, to let me down easy!

The most common coping mechanism is denial — where I simply do not see what I don't want to see, even if it's obvious to everyone else.

Other well-known coping mechanisms:

Avoidance: When I change the subject, pretend things are OK when they are not or postpone things indefinitely.

Projection: Attributing something I am feeling or doing to someone else. For example: a very jealous, possessive boyfriend might be cheating and projecting his infidelity onto me. Yep — we often accuse others of what we ourselves do.

Displacement: The redirection of a strong emotion to something that cannot hurt me. For example, I come home from a bad day at work and snap at my significant other.

Sublimation: This is the healthy version of displacement. For example, I am so angry I want to punch someone and immediately go take boxing lessons or pound the pavement.

Repression: Inability to remember painful events. I might have no memory of them but they can still have an impact on my life and why I do what I do.

Regression: Feeling scared or hurt and going back to something I found soothing when I was a kid. This is what I do when I seek comfort food or when I throw a tantrum. (Not that I would ever.)

Dissociation: When I lose track of time or of myself — I "disconnect" from the world and live in another that is less overwhelming.

Acting out: When instead of using my words I jump up and down, slam doors, throw things or punch a hole in the wall.

Rationalization: Attempting to excuse with facts something I know I should not have done. But, everybody does it!

Intellectualization: When my emotions feel overwhelmed and I respond by focusing on doing something rational. For example, I begin researching places I can stay when I leave my relationship, instead of grieving the loss.

Reaction formation: When I behave in a way that is inconsistent with how I feel — something terrible happens to me and I react to it with an excess of positivity.

Compartmentalization: Regarding my life as siloed instead of a whole so I can carry on with one silo even if the other seems to be falling apart. For example, I am going through a horrible breakup but I don't let it affect me at work.

Coping mechanisms are wonderful. They help me better manage the world and all the painful things in it — if I can't manage everything, then at least I can manage how I perceive it, right?

Except, after a while, acting in a way that is counter to reality catches up to me.

This is why learning about coping mechanisms is valuable: it's easier to become aware of things I know.

REGRESSION

PROJECTION

SUBLIMATION

DISPLACEMENT

AVOIDANCE

— YAY! I'M SAFE!

REPRESSION

THE BLACK HOLE OF REALITY

Pandemic Life Lessons

Nothing will go as expected.

Rejecting my feelings because someone has it worse is nonsensical.

I don't always have to look for the good.

The present moment is all I have.

I will practice surrendering to uncertainty and unpredictability.

I was never really in control.

Self-care is not an indulgence.

Sensorial pleasure is grounding.

Stillness is always good.

Exercise is essential.

Deep breaths are always good.

Sleeping is always good.

More time to read a real book is always good.

Asking *"What is this here to teach me?"* is always good.

Listening to music while doing nothing else is a luxury.

Thinking about how I can help feels better than thinking about how we are doomed.

Online activity: less panic, more things to learn.

Living in survival mode causes a stress response that affects my immune system.

We are one. We can't just act for ourselves.

Listen to science and data.

Flexibility is where it's at. The ability to throw out any plans or beliefs and start over.

The quicker you accept, the quicker you adapt.

Rethink "essential."

Any form of inequality eventually leads to a crumbling of the system.

We were doing too much.

We were not spending enough time with ourselves.

I still have most of what I've taken for granted.

How Can I "Parent" Myself?

Learn to recognize your needs. This typically requires spending time by yourself.

Find a quiet place and look at your thoughts. Look at your feelings. Without labeling anything as "good" or "bad", get a sense for what you are witnessing, as if you were outside yourself.

Determine what you need. You can give yourself what you need via two things: promises you make to yourself (to get where you want to go) and boundaries (to protect yourself from the demands of others).

Some examples of what you might need: a good night of sleep. Quiet time. A day off. Time connecting with a friend you haven't spoken to. A long walk. A difficult conversation.

Dedicate time to creating something.

Do something surprising. Routine, habits and rituals are important but so is stepping out of what you do every day to awaken your senses.

Give yourself what you expected a parent to give you. Validate yourself. Approve of yourself. Tell yourself what you would have liked to hear: I see you. I am listening. I believe you.

Listen to your inner voice and don't let her be critical of you. Replace judgment and criticism with love and support.

Do these last two points seem silly or ineffective? The more you practice, the more you show up for yourself, the more powerful your relationship with yourself will become.

Self-Compassion

The act of exercising self-compassion allows me to see things more clearly. Let me give you some examples:

With no self-compassion, I believe I have to turn my back on anything I need to make another person the priority. With self-compassion, I can see that taking care of myself and caring for others do not have to be at odds with each other. I can be a caring person, which includes being caring with me.

With no self-compassion, I believe a volatile, roller coaster of a relationship is unpredictable and passionate. With self-compassion, I recognize that "reliable" and "steady" are incredibly sexy qualities and that my addiction to drama is setting my filter wrong.

With no self-compassion, I believe setting boundaries is a form of betrayal — that loyalty is saying yes to everything. With self-compassion, I understand that as a human I have limits, and that relationships become healthier if I express them.

With no self-compassion, I interpret the boundaries of others as a form of rejection and I experience this rejection over and over. With self-compassion I can see that another person saying *"I want to be alone this weekend"* is them wanting time with themselves, rather than them not wanting to be with me.

Insecurity distorts the world, causing me pain. The antidote to this distortion is to be kind to myself.

Comfortable Being Uncomfortable

I don't ever get comfortable with being uncomfortable. Rather, I come to terms with discomfort as the price to pay if I want to grow.

I remind myself that —

If I am uncomfortable I will make my comfort zone bigger.

Just because something doesn't feel right does not mean I should avoid it.

Just because I don't like doing something does not mean I should never do it.

Just because I am afraid or nervous is not enough of a reason not to try it.

Just because something is difficult doesn't mean I should run from it.

Just because I have never done something doesn't mean I shouldn't try it.

Just because something is going to suck doesn't mean it won't be valuable.

Just because something is risky doesn't mean it's not worth doing.

I tell myself *"this will be awful and that is OK."*

This is the logic I use when I have difficult conversations, when I try something new, when I leave a job I know for a job I don't, when I tell someone how I feel, when I deem it important to go to a social event and would rather stay home, when I do things that would be easier for me not to do (such as accept a speaking opportunity), and when I set a boundary that makes me feel like I am being selfish.

After doing something hard I always feel proud of whatever discomfort I overcame.

Things I'm Less Interested In

Seeing anything as a dichotomy.

Attempting to affect the outcome.

Getting you to see things my way.

Trying to please somebody.

Trying to get someone else to change.

Going to anyone for advice.

Bending in an attempt to be anything I am not.

Waiting.

Trying to forget.

Listening to my ego.

Winning an argument.

Explaining myself.

Blaming others.

Being goal oriented.

Being future oriented.

Amassing possessions.

Dwelling on fear, regret or disappointment.

Calling people "mine".

Insisting anyone do anything my way.

Looking for things I had expected to find.

Any effort expended to get anything to remain the same.

Getting everything perfect.

Any form of competition.

Drama.

Worrying about what others think of me.

Complaining.

Holding on to anything heavy. Anger. Resentment. Shoes that never really fit.

Benefits of Setting Boundaries

The first step towards setting boundaries has to do with listening to me, being connected to myself, being clear on what I want. Boundaries are identity.

When I set good boundaries and protect them — recognizing all the while that the best boundaries are elastic — I show myself I can trust me. I prove to me I will stand up for me. Boundaries are self-respect, self-esteem and confidence. Boundaries are self-love.

When my limits are clear, my relationships are healthier. Boundaries improve my ability to relate to others.

When others can see and respect my boundaries, I feel less anger, less bitterness, less resentment, less disappointment. Boundaries are peace and happiness.

My time, my energy, my body and my things are protected and safe, and I can use all these things in a more deliberate way rather than squandering them on things I am not really interested in doing. Boundaries are purpose.

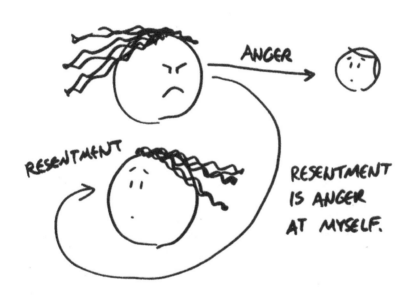

ANGER

RESENTMENT

RESENTMENT
IS ANGER
AT MYSELF.

Safety First and Other Tips

Safety first. Yes, you only live once. So maybe don't do anything that would put your one life at risk.

Love yourself. Your feelings about you are the lens through which you see the world. Your insecurities will sink you.

Tell the truth. If you can't, then whatever you are doing is a bad idea.

Don't be nervous. Everyone thinks everyone is looking at them.

Be a beginner, an amateur, rather than trying to demonstrate how much you know.

Take classes you know nothing about rather than classes likely to be easy.

Put yourself in a position where you learn more about a variety of things. Some people thrive by specialization — narrowing down their expertise. You (Dushka), thrive by variety and that will serve you well forever.

Exercise. Every day. It's for your brain.

Don't ever underestimate the importance of friendship. That friend will outlast that boy by decades.

Don't ever underestimate the importance of sleep.

Don't ever underestimate the importance of eating well.

Don't underestimate the power of beauty. Get fresh flowers. Go to museums.

Expose yourself to art and to nature.

Don't overestimate the importance of stuff. You don't really need that. Travel light.

Read. Write. Every single thing you do you will do better if you are well read and a good writer.

Practice presenting. Being a good presenter is a life skill.

Forget about *"I don't know what I want to do when I grow up"*. Whatever sparks your interest is the way.

Why Is It Hard To Know Oneself?

Because if I am not used to it, spending time alone is full of sharp, serrated edges.

Because if I am unaccustomed to it, silence can seem oppressive.

Because my brain confuses who I am with who I should be.

Because my brain confuses who I am with who I want to be.

Because it's hard to distinguish what I want from what others want for me.

Because it's hard to distinguish what I want from what others want from me.

Because it's hard to recognize that what works for "everyone" doesn't work for me.

Because what I am good at gets approval so I forget that just because I am good at it doesn't mean it's what I want to do.

Because I believe that what other people say about me defines me.

Because I believe that how other people behave towards me defines me.

Because the insignificant, everyday things distract me from thinking about the big things.

Because I place more value on getting approval so I do what I think you want rather than even identify what I want.

Because looking at myself can be scary so I avoid it.

Small Changes, Big Impact

Pick up a healthy habit, keep it small, and never skip it. For example, add a 30 minute walk to any part of your day. You will improve your health, clear your thoughts — but most importantly, begin to teach yourself that you can be trusted with what you promise yourself you will do.

Download a meditation app. My favorite is Calm (I don't work for them or represent them). It's helped me sleep better, be more mindful, and helps me manage anxiety.

While you are at it, do what you need to do to improve your sleep. Everything is better if you sleep well. Everything.

Clean up your social media. Remove from your feed anything that makes you feel like everyone else's life is better than yours and carefully pick what inspires you, uplifts you, teaches you. If you are going to expose yourself to something every day, make it preposterously enriching.

While you are cleaning up your feed, connect with a good friend you haven't seen in way too long, preferably in person.

Spend more time outside.

Deep Self-Care

I am aware of my inner critic. *"Hey, Dushka, can you lower your voice? I'm trying to get work done over here."*

I tell the truth as often and as clearly as possible.

I listen to my feelings instead of telling myself I shouldn't feel them.

I take responsibility.

I assume the best in others.

I express my limits and respect the limits of others.

I keep the promises I make to myself.

If I don't keep them I forgive myself and quickly begin again.

I feed curiosity.

I create habits and rituals and believe everything is a practice.

I ask for what I need.

I examine criticism rather than swallowing it whole.

I am comfortable disappointing others.

I remind myself things can always get better, even when they are already really good.

I don't believe in jinxes and do believe in celebrating prematurely.

I celebrate effort, not just results.

I make sleep a priority.

I spend time alone.

I identify what is bad for me and step away.

I remind myself that trying to change someone else is self-destructive.

I am not daunted by "awkward".

I question what I believe.

I watch my ego. She is so creative.

I spin best-case scenarios instead of worst-case scenarios. Both leave me unprepared, but one is way more fun.

I write every day.

I believe in magic.

I SPIN BEST CASE SCENARIOS,

NOT...

WORST CASE.

BOTH LEAVE ME UNPREPARED, BUT ONE IS MORE FUN.

LZDR

89

What if I Never Leave My Comfort Zone?

You will find yourself with a routine that becomes stale.

A life that feels confined.

An absence of thrill.

Mediocrity.

Stagnation.

Boredom.

Loss of drive.

Loss of creativity.

Loss of imagination.

Loss of inspiration.

Loss of self-esteem.

Never experiencing anything new.

Never learning anything new.

Inability to feel pleasure.

Wondering. What if?

Never knowing what you could have been.

Mistakes To Make

Get everything perfect.

Blame.

Be a victim.

Lie.

Play it safe.

Settle.

Live the life someone else wants for you.

People please.

Fail to set boundaries.

Ignore your gut.

Trust your gut, believing "our gut is never wrong".

Attempt to arrive at a different result by following the same patterns.

Fall in love with the wrong person.

Stay in a relationship that cannot be repaired.

Trust the wrong person.

Get your heart broken.

Never give up.

Wait.

Refuse to change your mind.

Consider everyone a competitor.

Take the wrong job.

Cut the line.

Burn out.

Burn a bridge.

Refuse to get old.

Risk everything and lose.

Overestimate yourself.

Underestimate yourself.

Social Norms

Social norms have a way of disconnecting us from ourselves. Here are some examples:

Allowing *"what will everyone think of me?"* to guide what I do or don't do. (Following through on a wedding despite my sense of doom, because the invitations have already been sent out.)

Keeping myself busy so I can seem important, instead of listening to when I need to slow down, pause, think, rest, lounge, loiter.

Feeling like failing or quitting is not an option — when failing is part of any learning process, indivisible from true progress, and quitting is often the healthy (and sane) course of action.

Choosing a profession — doctor, lawyer — that is not at all what I want, and wondering why I feel listless and empty at the end of a grueling day.

Believing that putting myself first is "selfish" instead of healthy, and that "sacrifice" is virtuous, necessary and a sign of loyalty, then wondering why I so often feel taken advantage of.

Refraining from saying "no" in an effort to not seem rude or off-putting, then having to deal with overwhelming resentment when I find myself doing things I don't want to do.

Spending money on things I cannot afford — an expensive car, an expensive house, an expensive wedding — in an effort to make an impression.

Presenting myself a certain way on social media, to contribute to the sowing of a collective sense of inadequacy, instead of using social media as a way to connect with people who feel all the things I feel. Connection is better than envy, but then I'd have to admit my life is not perfect and that sometimes I too feel lost.

Ah.
Thursday
veggies...

How To Grow

Learn new things.

Play.

Create something.

Feed curiosity.

Question my thoughts.

Question my beliefs.

Give up being right.

Recognize more than one reality.

Recognize emotions as fleeting.

Distinguish my ego from me.

Distinguish real from the story.

It's not about me.

Practice setting and respecting boundaries.

Follow through on what I say I'm going to do.

Ask *"what is this here to teach me?"*

Relinquish control.

Get comfortable being misunderstood.

Get comfortable disappointing others.

Get comfortable with change.

Accept.

Surrender.

Spend time alone.

It's not about "growth." It's about learning how to love myself.

How Do I Avoid Mistakes?

Do nothing.

Try nothing.

Learn nothing.

Venture nothing.

Risk nothing.

Move nothing.

Anticipate every possible worst-case scenario.

Spend all your time making meticulous plans you never put into action because of the importance of my next point:

Never put anything into action.

When you do make a mistake, berate yourself to ensure you never make it again.

Alternative: before you have followed any of these steps realize that living a life focused on not making mistakes is no way to live.

Was That a Positive Experience?

I would consider something a positive experience if:

I wanted to tell everyone about it.

I felt an urge to recommend it.

I felt joyful, exhilarated, expansive, awakened.

If it granted me a sense of abundance.

If it made me laugh.

If it filled me with gratitude.

If it made me feel fortunate.

If I felt awe.

If I felt overcome by ataraxia, even for a moment.

If it resulted in me feeling madly curious and wanting to know more.

If it made me feel like I was a beginner, wondrous.

If it shifted my perception, leaving me with a new perspective.

If it made me feel proud of what I'd done.

If the outcome was related to my resilience or evolution.

If I learned something new.

If I felt more connected.

If it left me feeling moved, inspired.

If looking back on the experience makes me smile.

If I wish I could do it again.

Things That Seem Good but Are Not

Expecting to have it all together.

Getting things perfect.

Multitasking.

What feels familiar.

Refusing to make mistakes.

Refusing to ask for help.

Needing to be happy all the time.

Striving to make others happy.

Being too demanding of myself.

Being critical of myself.

Trying to change another person.

Trying to control another person.

Unrealistic expectations.

Unrealistic goals.

Equating longevity with a successful relationship.

Exacting revenge.

Refusing to accept what is.

What Makes People Powerful?

Action, rather than inactivity. The realization it's action that begets motivation, not the other way around.

The hunger for learning new things. The more I learn, the more capable I become.

Making decisions for myself instead of the limbo of waiting for someone else to decide something for me.

Setting boundaries instead of looking to others for approval. Setting boundaries instead of pretending to agree. Setting boundaries instead of letting others run my life.

The willingness to make decisions that disappoint others, or that others don't like.

A sense of purpose.

Taking responsibility. Blame is a quick recipe to powerlessness.

The change in perspective from feeling like I'm stuck to realizing that I can make a choice or a series of choices to get unstuck. It's not easy, but instead of feeling hopeless, instead of settling, I can plot my escape.

Imaginary Limits

I am not good enough.

I am not whatever enough.

I don't have what it takes.

He is better than me.

She is better than me.

Everyone else is better than me.

Everyone knows something I don't know.

I am going to fall flat on my face.

I don't have time.

I don't know enough.

I don't deserve whatever.

I am an impostor.

Everyone will know I have nothing to offer.

Why would anyone care about what I have to say?

I'm too weird.

I'm not creative.

I'm not organized.

I'm not cool.

I'm not motivated.

I don't want to sell out.

I'm too young.

I'm too old.

I will look like an idiot.

I am insecure.

I am shy.

I can't. I just can't.

What's the point?

There is no point.

What am I even doing with my life?

I don't belong here.

I don't belong anywhere.

Nobody likes me.

Nobody believes in me.

I don't believe in myself.

I don't know how to believe in myself.

Tell me how. How can I learn to believe in myself?

What Should I Do if I Can't Sleep?

When I am feeling anxious and can't fall asleep:

I get out of bed.

I keep the lights on low.

I walk around.

I appeal to all my senses in an effort to get out of my head and into my body. Smell something. See something. Touch something. Hear something. Taste something.

I consider what else I can do to feel better, such as taking a hot bath or playing relaxing music.

With a notebook in hand, I feel around for the shape of my anxiety. Is it specific? General? Is it distorting things, making them up or making them bigger than they are?

I ask myself how I got here. Have I been taking care of myself, eating well, sleeping well?

Can I list all the times my anxiety has lied to me, has told me there was no way out and there was?

Is there someone I can talk to? Or, can I talk to me? If I was my friend telling me about my anxiety, what would I tell her?

106

What can I do for myself now that might help me in the future?
I take notes for her. Take out the clothes for her to wear
tomorrow to make the morning as easy as I can.

There is something about present day me taking care of future
me that I find reassuring, and hopeful.

Emotional Maturity

To any degree, practice:

More responsibility, less blame.

More truth-telling, less truth-smudging.

More boundaries, less people-pleasing.

More awareness regarding what I need, less pushing aside what I need.

More validating myself, less expecting others to validate me.

More self-care, less dismissing it as "selfish."

More self-compassion, less berating myself.

More forgiving, less grudges.

More self-forgiving, less regret.

More awareness of my patterns, less falling into them.

More pausing, less reacting.

More "this is not about me", less me-centric.

More asking, less assuming.

More self-evaluation, less judgment of others.

More surrender, less control.

More flexibility, less rigidity.

More resilience, less despair.

More self-trust, less self-doubt.

More learning, less coasting.

More acceptance, less inner war.

Worst-Case Scenario

The first step necessary for me to stop spinning worst-case scenarios is to let go of the notion that "they prepare me". How can I refrain from doing something if I believe it assists in my survival?

The second step is, I present to my catastrophic alter ego equally plausible, wonderful scenarios.

"What if that thing ends up being a disaster?" she says. *"Well,"* I say. *"What if it ends up being amazing?"*

"What if nobody likes me?" she says. *"Well,"* I say, *"It's more likely they are worried about nobody liking them than they are thinking about you."*

"What if I am not good enough?" she says. *"What if you are flawed, but awesome?"* I say.

"Not worrying feels like I am doing nothing," she says. *"Worrying full time is the same as doing nothing,"* I say.

Then, I periodically take stock of how things went once they are in the past. I confirm that most of my worst-case scenarios do not ever take place and that I ruin one moment after another spinning out over things that never happen.

Mistakes I Never Stop Making

I keep forgetting feelings are temporary. When I feel blue I'm convinced it will never get better.

I take things personally. When I have not heard from a friend in what feels like a long time I am certain they don't love me anymore and often they are just busy.

I forget about boundaries and say yes to things I should have said no to.

I berate myself, like — *"Dushka, my god you should know better"* — and forget I should treat myself with compassion. I'd never tell a friend *"My god Petronia, you should know better!"*

I ferociously protect myself against non-existent threats.

I find myself hyper-focused on the emotional state of another person completely forgetting that their emotional state is not something I need to (or can) manage.

I forget to feel curious and instead feel defensive.

I forget to identify what I need and realize I haven't had water for hours or that I'm not making sleep a priority. Then I wonder why I'm so tired.

I confuse my ego with me and make suboptimal decisions.

I feel pressured by other people's expectations of me.

I believe my own stories.

I define things as "insurmountable" completely forgetting I've gotten myself through a whole lot worse.

Self-Confidence

Self-confidence is the process by which you prove to yourself you can be counted on.

You witness yourself making difficult decisions and value the process more than the outcome.

You witness yourself doing things that scare you and learn you can do them right through the fear.

You witness yourself doing hard things: making a choice that is right, even if the wrong choice is of greater benefit to you.

You make promises to yourself and you keep them, even if keeping them demands a sacrifice.

You falter and fail yourself and instead of perpetual discouragement you offer yourself compassion, shake it off and begin again.

Life Lessons I Learn but Forget

Any clasping around the way I wanted something to be is not helpful.

Worry is not just useless but destructive.

Surrender is strength, not weakness.

The only thing that's real is now.

A positive outcome is always plausible.

Feelings cannot be dismissed.

Forced optimism is an act of self-aggression.

Fear is ravenous and will become insatiable if you feed it.

Pain always feels like it will never get better.

Insurmountable

I have overcome many things I was certain were insurmountable. During those times:

I thought about how I might break the insurmountable thing into smaller, more manageable pieces.

I took things one moment, one day at a time.

I reminded myself that just because I have no idea exactly how something will work out doesn't mean it won't.

I learned about perseverance (doing one tiny bit every day, inching towards resolution) and about surrender (recognizing that resolution was not within my power and that letting it go would be more helpful than fighting a battle I had no agency over).

I witnessed that many, many times insurmountable things resolve themselves.

I noticed I underestimate my own resilience and adaptability and remind myself about this the next time I am before something unsurmountable.

The fact is this: many things are in fact insurmountable. These, by definition, cannot be overcome.

But many, many things I with certainty classified as such were really not.

The Meaning of an Open Mind

I am comfortable when I don't know.

I am comfortable when I'm wrong.

Instead of listening only to people who already think like I think, I am able to listen to people who think differently from how I think.

I am receptive to new ideas, even hungry or curious for more.

I ask a lot of questions (which come from attempting to process information I am ignorant about), rather than jumping to conclusions (which come from what I already believe).

I change my mind.

119

Tell the Truth

Here is a sure-fire way to change your life: tell the truth.

What would this look like?

First, I abandon the notion that truth-telling needs to be tactless or brutal. It does not, and the onus is on me to figure this out.

Then:

I start with me. In this truth-telling process, I learn how to tell myself the truth.

No denial.

No excuses.

No protecting myself against a truth I find uncomfortable.

No casting blame to avoid responsibility, not even to say *"I'm stuck in traffic"* when I should have left earlier.

No using a lie as a path of least resistance. No saying I'm fine if I'm not.

No justifying another person's behavior.

No eating the piece of cake with the most icing and hoping no one will notice.

No pretending I don't know why another person is hurt.

No using my powers to convince others of something I know is not true.

No using my powers to convince myself of something more pleasant than the truth.

No insincerity, such as failing to follow through or failing to live up to commitments or promises.

No flaky behavior — no last minute canceling or failing to show up when I said I would.

No acting inconsistently or unpredictably.

No bluffing, not even to win at poker.

No hypocrisy.

No double standards.

No lies by omission. I cannot lie by leaving out critical information.

No passive deception.

No distortions.

No duplicity. This also means no gossip, no criticism, no judging others.

No minimization.

No exaggeration.

No gaslighting. ("*I didn't mean it that way! Don't be so sensitive!*")

No fabrications.

No plagiarizing or taking credit for work I didn't do.

No white lies or telling myself this is the kind thing to do and this lie doesn't count because whatever.

No lies to cover lies I already told. No covering my tracks.

No saying one thing and doing another.

No lies told by my actions. No attending events I don't want to be at, spending time with people I don't really want to spend time with, no saying yes when I mean no, no saying no when I mean yes.

No pretending. No pretending I like people I don't like or pretending I like my job if I don't. This does not give me license to be hurtful. It just means I step away from anything that requires me to misrepresent anything.

My bet is that a strict "tell the truth" practice will change my life, and I bet it would do the same for you.

Things That Reduce Your Quality of Life

The sense that what I need and want is always somewhere else. Or, put another way, the belief that I have to somehow go find something meant for me.

Hunger for control.

An absence of attention.

A loud, relentless inner critic.

Noise.

Sleep deprivation.

Procrastination.

Comparison.

Suspicion.

Worry.

Cynicism.

Blame.

Settling.

Holding a grudge.

Avoiding or postponing something because it's difficult.

Expectations and disappointment (they go hand in hand).

Resentment. (This is a symptom of poor boundaries.)

Being hooked on external validation.

Taking responsibility for things that I am not responsible for (such as how someone else behaves).

The assumption that I have to work hard at getting someone to love me.

Not Worth the Effort

Always being right.

Proving others wrong.

Debating.

Attempting to control others.

Managing what others think of me.

Staying "on top of" social media.

Judging rather than identifying what I need to change about myself.

Saying yes when I want to say no.

Getting approval.

Small talk.

Complaining.

A relationship that's run its course.

Getting another to meet my needs.

Living up to another's expectations.

Playing any role someone else gave me.

Fixing another.

Time I spend with someone I don't love.

Resentment.

Keeping a secret.

Protecting a lie.

Keeping score.

Holding a grudge.

Plotting revenge.

Living with suspicion.

Assuming the worst.

Spinning up worst-case scenarios.

Reacting, instead of pausing.

Jumping to conclusions.

Procrastinating.

Feeling like I'm always behind.

Things Someone Should Teach Us

Boundaries. You can say no. You don't have to betray yourself to love or be loved.

Spending time alone is indispensable.

Self-care is not a luxury.

Sleep is not a waste of time.

You can regulate yourself with your breath, available to you any time.

You can do better by doing less. Less control. Less "helping". Less worry. Less guilt.

You are supposed to question your own thoughts.

What other people do or say does not define you. Someone not loving you is not related to your lovability.

Recognize all the lies your ego tells you. Ego is the opposite of peace.

You get to decide who to surround yourself with.

Being misunderstood or being disappointing is inevitable.

The importance of first identifying, then clearly expressing what you want.

You can give yourself everything you need.

Humans want to be heard. Heard without anyone needing to do anything other than listening. No fixing, no giving advice, no judging, no trying to control them or the outcome. I hear you. I see you.

Tired and True

Know yourself.

Love yourself.

Everything you need is already inside of you.

Believe in you.

You won't always get what you want.

One step at a time.

Don't worry about what others think.

Learn to listen.

You become like the people you surround yourself with.

Develop a gratitude practice.

Forgive.

Read.

Don't ever stop learning.

Be kind.

As you give to the world, the world gives to you.

131

Reasons I Feel Lost

Most common reasons why I regularly feel lost:

Because I have put my life in someone else's hands. I've been listening to others regarding the choices I should be making, except, the only one who has to live with my choices is me.

Because I have lost touch with how to listen to myself.

Because I've convinced myself that what I want does not make sense.

Because I feel like I don't know what I want.

Because I have changed and what I want has changed (pro tip: this means every one of us has a recurring sense of feeling lost, not just me).

Because I have come to believe the solution to feeling lost is something drastic like taking a trip somewhere remote to "find myself", when the truth is big change is accomplished right here, right now, with small steps that become habits.

Small, everyday habits to counteract the sense that I am lost:

Notice. Am I doing this in an effort to get someone to like me or think highly of me or because I really want to?

Have I outlined clear boundaries? Learning to say no even if it feels "selfish" (it's not) helps me identify who I am and what I want.

Am I spending enough time with myself? If I am always surrounded by others I cannot hear myself.

I don't need to identify grand, life altering passions. But, what am I curious about? What makes me feel intrigued? What feels less boring? What doesn't make me feel dread?

Can I get up every morning and do something for my health? Eat better, exercise regularly? I can't feel found if I am not connected to my body.

Do I have a practice of self-love? This is how I learn to believe in myself, trust my own feelings, stand up for what I want and accept where I am at. It's perfectly OK — normal! natural! — for me to feel repeatedly lost, and finding my way is part of what makes life an adventure.

ME,
LOST

MYSELF,
RIGHT HERE!

DZDR

Big Things That Take 10 Minutes

Deep breaths. Yoga. A ten minute walk. Ten minutes of writing. A ten minute call with a friend. Tea.

I clean my space and as I do I feel my brain unwinding.

I organize my calendar (and take out a thing or two).

I do one thing at a time. Multitasking is self-neglect.

I keep a promise I made to myself.

I get something done that I've been putting off.

I have a difficult conversation I've been avoiding.

I clear up a misunderstanding.

I swap being unclear for a boundary. *"I don't know if I can"* becomes *"I am overcommitted but thank you for thinking of me".*

I feel proud of myself for doing the thing or having the talk or setting the boundary.

I course correct a negative thought. (It's not that this person doesn't care about me — it's that they are really busy.)

I take a nap. I don't need to earn it.

I Don't Know What To Do With My Life

You will never know what to do with your life.

You don't really know what you want.

The time when you get things figured out does not exist.

Life is not about finding your purpose but about stumbling along doing things you find interesting and witnessing your purpose create itself. In other words, purpose is an accident.

Most of the things you believe are cognitive distortions. The most useful skill you can develop is learning how to question your own thoughts.

While you are at it, question your fears. The more you understand them the better because you are the creator of the things you fear the most.

Life is really tough and no one owes you anything. Think hard about what you owe yourself.

Life is not fair. Believing it should be is an illusion (actually, it's another cognitive distortion).

Many times, the difference between *"everything is an adventure"* and *"I am in a panic because everything is uncertain"* is how you interpret it.

Less control, more surrender.

Become a passionate believer in luck and in serendipity. You cannot detect what you deny.

Learn to love yourself. If you don't, you will be perpetually lost at sea.

Take care of your body. It really is your temple. Also, use it in all the delicious ways nature intended.

Never underestimate the magical power of sleep.

Decide that you want to be happy and keep in mind, every time you think the other shoe is going to drop, every time you think that maybe you don't deserve it, that there is no limit to how happy you can be.

Things That Help Me Find Peace

Living in the present.

Taking things one moment at a time.

Equanimity: the practice of regarding any situation as a neutral situation without qualifying it as good or bad. It's related to "this too will pass".

Recognizing we are separate from our thoughts and that not all they think is true.

The understanding that things we consider implausible are plausible, which applies to bad scenarios, but equally to good scenarios.

Feelings That Are Universal

I feel lonely but also I am convinced no one else feels this way.

I have no purpose.

I am worthless.

I am unlovable.

I am trapped.

I want to escape this life and start over somewhere far away.

I am sad.

I am anxious.

I feel grief.

I feel shame.

I don't understand what's wrong with me.

Everyone else is better than me.

Everyone else has figured out something I am in the dark about.

I want what someone else has (envy).

Someone will take away something that is mine (jealousy).

People think I'm good at X and instead I am an impostor.

Someone else can save me.

I can fix someone else.

My life has no meaning.

As a result of these universal emotions, I ask myself — if everyone feels someone else is better, if we all feel someone else has figured it out, if we are all lonely, does it not stand to reason our feelings might be deceiving us?

YOU ARE NOT ALONE

How Do I Live a Simple Life?

Bask in doing nothing.

Believe that less is more.

Slow down.

Pause before you react.

Focus on what you have = practice gratitude.

Practice setting boundaries. Saying no declutters a complicated life.

How other people behave says nothing about you. You don't need to make excuses for them, solve, convince, persuade, push or cajole.

You cannot get another person to love you.

You cannot help, save or rescue another.

Live below your means. This does not imply deprivation.

Stop owning or buying things you don't really need.

Stop chasing.

Reduce possessions.

Reduce consumption.

Favor experiences over stuff. Stuff becomes clutter. Experiences become memories.

Be clean and organized.

Eat food that is not processed.

Don't inflict on yourself a packed schedule.

Focus on one thing at a time.

What Seems Sad but Isn't?

No one is coming to save you.

No one has the answers to your pressing life questions.

It is not possible to fix somebody else.

When it comes to figuring yourself out, only you can do that.

Love does not conquer all.

You won't always be happy.

Soulmates do not exist.

Your feelings will change.

Your thoughts lie to you.

Your perception is not reality.

Not loving yourself distorts every experience.

Your expectations will sink you.

You will betray yourself.

Nothing is yours to keep.

The meaning of life is for you to decide.

Signs You Are Growing Up

You like being alone.

You are at peace with silence.

You are centered in the midst of conflict.

You have stopped blaming others.

You are less defensive.

You listen without waiting for your turn to talk.

You step away from anything that is not good for you.

You are less concerned with "awkward".

You rest and you push yourself when you need to and experience less difficulty telling the difference.

You stop running from feeling things that are painful. If you are sad, you are sad rather than sad being something that needs fixing.

You recognize grief without declaring it doesn't make sense.

You accept emotions without feeling they need a why.

Your inner dialogue is improving. That was really hard and you did it!

You are more deliberate about where your time goes.

You don't expect anyone to come to your rescue.

The sense that you're all you've got is a reason to rejoice rather than feel bereft.

You keep the promises you make to yourself which also means you take care of yourself.

You've stopped judging others. How can you, if you too have your story?

You have clear boundaries and are increasingly comfortable establishing them.

You are much less worried about what others think when you set these boundaries.

You respect the boundaries of those around you.

There is a gap of time, a breath or two between action and reaction.

You listen without trying to fix things and refrain from giving advice. Fixing things — *"don't be sad!"* — is about you. What the other is telling you about is space for them.

You communicate and ask questions rather than jumping to conclusions.

You get that it's not all about you.

You suffer less.

Your goals, objectives and vows are both sacred and elastic. This duality is difficult, like something that shifts in and out of focus. Holding duality, ambiguity, seemingly contradictory things — I am right and wrong, happy and anxious, lost and proud — defines what it means to grow up.

To Learn As Early as Possible

Don't wait. It's not a virtue.

Don't rush. Your life has its own cadence and you should trust it.

Learn everything you can about boundaries. Setting them, protecting them, respecting those of others.

People-pleasing is a quick way to lose yourself.

You should stay away from anyone who is not good for you, in particular anyone who makes you feel you have to work at getting them to love you. Love is not the result of effort. Love is free.

Perfectionism is overrated.

Both praise and criticism should be taken with a grain of salt.

Your ego and other voices, such as your anxiety, regularly lie to you. Learn to observe and question your own thoughts.

Many things we believe are "personality" are habits.

Practice means you can accomplish many things you thought you never could.

Discipline is how you develop character.

Keeping the promises you make to yourself will teach you that you are the person you can trust the most.

Anything you do every day will add up. This alone makes me feel like the world is filled with magic.

Feelings are fleeting. If you feel awful (or amazing) you won't feel like this forever. Despair comes from the lie that is believing this is how things will be from now on.

On a related note, everything is impermanent. Don't believe anything is yours to keep.

Just because something works for everyone doesn't mean it will work for you. Don't go looking for "normal."

There is nothing wrong with you.

Taking care of yourself is neither indulgent nor selfish. (Pro tip: when someone calls you selfish it's because you are doing what you want, not what they want. In other words, it's an indication they are the ones thinking of themselves.)

The love of your life is you.

Why Is It Hard To Express Feelings?

Because not every feeling has a word.

Because I don't know. I don't know how I feel.

Because what I feel makes no sense.

Because what I feel is contradictory.

Because I shouldn't be feeling this.

Because I am the only one who has ever felt this way.

Because I am afraid.

Because I don't trust you.

Because I want you to know how I feel without having to tell you.

Because if I tell you how I feel you might think less of me.

Because, what for, if it never helps?

Because I don't deserve getting what I need.

Because you might stop loving me.

Because you might not like me.

Because it would make me feel exposed.

Because you would think I'm weak.

Because I don't want to fight.

Because I don't want to get hurt.

Because I don't want to hurt you.

Because I'd end up alone.

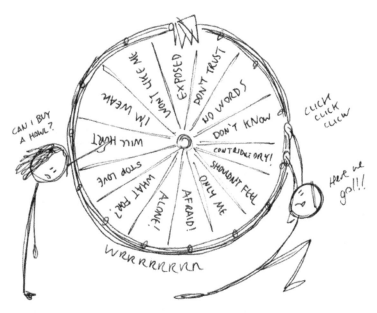

WHEEL OF UNEXPRESSED FEELINGS

Inevitable

Everything will change.

You will outgrow people important to you.

You will love the wrong person.

You will be the wrong person.

You will lose whatever you think belongs to you.

You will feel lost.

Things will end.

You will fight.

You will make mistakes.

You will experience regret.

You will experience unhappiness.

You will take something incredibly valuable for granted.

You will experience injustice.

You will experience astounding good fortune.

You will seize opportunity.

You will miss opportunities.

You will witness something "unsolvable" resolve itself.

You will fail.

You will not know what to do.

You will be afraid.

Time will pass. As it does it will feel slow. As you look back you will wonder where it went.

You will get old — every part of you that is now spry, supple, nimble, springy and lustrous will get brittle, creaky, rigid, unyielding, dull. But only if you are lucky.

Things That Make You Unhappy

A resolve to get everything perfect.

A sense that I need to and should control everything.

Comparing anything beautiful that I have to anything another has or seems to have.

Pretending. It's hard to fix, address or mend anything I am pretending does not exist.

Lying. It feels like it helps but only for a single moment. After that, it's just a labyrinth creator.

Spending time with anything or anyone who drains me of all life force.

Waiting. In particular waiting for things to change, waiting for things to get better or waiting for an apology.

Neglecting to spend time with myself to the point I am neglecting me.

An imperative to be right.

A sense that I have to know everything.

Insisting that I'm OK and that everything is fine when it's not.

Ignoring how I feel = me ignoring me.

Saying nothing when someone I love hurts my feelings because I know they didn't really mean it or they are having a bad day.

Putting off a difficult conversation until things become such a morass I don't even know where to start.

Settling.

Making a huge effort to be available to everyone all of the time.

Striving to get another's approval.

The belief I can convince another that I am worth being loved.

Spending time managing what other people think of me.

Feeling like happiness is just on the other side of ___.

Listening to various voices that come from inside of me and that lie to me, such as *"I will never get this right"* or *"I really should be over that"* or *"I should have known better."*

The fear that I will lose something I love.

The terror that someone I love will suffer.

Any form of self-punishment. It's a lot more effective to forgive myself, and to love myself.

Summary: it's me. I make me unhappy.

Negative Mindset

I will never be enough.

I will never have enough.

I am afraid.

I don't want anything to change.

This feeling that I'm feeling I will feel forever.

Everything is a competition.

I am better/less than you.

I am always right.

Everything is someone else's fault.

I am a victim.

If I am in a good place, my brain thinks the following thoughts:

I feel grateful.

I trust that change is something I can navigate.

I dig learning new things.

Feelings are fleeting.

I can create a better life through the decisions that I make.

OR

How Can I Validate Myself?

"Wow, Dushka. I did not think you'd get through the day, and you did it."

"You know what? You were right to be angry."

"Dushka, you did the best you could with what you knew."

"Setting that boundary was not easy, and it needed to be done."

"I know you're really upset Dushka so let's take some time to figure out what we need."

"I am really proud of you because what you did took courage, even if it didn't turn out the way you wanted it to."

"I think it's normal to sometimes agree to doing something you don't want to do and we will try to practice better boundaries again tomorrow."

Worth the Effort

Life.

Love.

Relationships.

Friendship.

Difficult conversations.

Facing fear.

Getting through "awkward" instead of cowering from it.

Telling the truth (not the white lie).

The creation of habits.

Meditation.

Getting up early.

Returning to a practice.

A shower.

Dressing up.

Straightening up. The procurement of a clean, well-lit space.

Good food.

Using a bowl, a napkin and silverware rather than the take-out container.

Learning something new.

Changing my mind.

Finding the right words. Expressing myself clearly and learning to ask for what I want.

Creativity: making room to write (or anything I love).

Spending time alone.

Getting to know me.

Going for a long walk.

Stopping to say hello to every pup.

Anything I do to take care of myself.

Questioning everything.

Questioning my own thoughts.

Looking for things I'm grateful for, in particular when I can't think of any.

Surrender.

Learning how to say no. It's really hard. It's so worth it.

WORTH THE EFFORT

Someday We Will Understand

It's not just that you are enough. You are so much more.

You are worth loving.

Most things are not about you, even when they feel deeply personal.

Another person's actions, behavior or opinions say nothing about you.

Most things change even when they feel permanent.

"Purpose" is not something you go looking for.

Soulmates are not something you wait for.

Feelings are like the weather. It's not that they are not real. It's that they are fleeting.

Your own thoughts lie to you in an attempt to keep you safe.

What sinks most relationships is our expectations.

You have less of what you chase.

Blame is a decoy.

Nothing is yours to keep.

You are beautiful.

Why Are People Controlling?

Because I want to make sure nothing can hurt me.

Because, if I dominate everything — the people around me, the outcome, the environment — I will know what to do.

Because I don't trust myself to get through uncertainty or change.

Controlling others is not a choice but a compulsion, not something I do out of pleasure but because I can't not.

I do it because I am afraid.

How To Keep Mentally Healthy

Start by practicing boundaries. No more people pleasing. No relating self-sacrifice with loyalty. No resentment or bitterness. Kindness begins by being kind to myself.

Notice. What is going on around me? What is going on inside of me? Can I practice awareness without drawing conclusions about what I see? Can I say things like *"Oh, I'm tired!"* without saying *"Why? Why are you so tired? Why can't you be stronger, more resilient?"* Abandon judgment.

Find the witness. Is that story my story or is that my ego? Is that thought I am thinking true? Is that feeling feeling like it will last forever? Find the witness: the person who thinks your thoughts and feels your feelings and listens to you and determines what is best for you. This person is never, not ever, anyone other than you.

Accept. This is where I am. This is where I start from. No more resisting reality which is an enormous waste of precious energy, because, alas. Reality is not going to budge as a result of me not wanting to see it.

Pause. Pause before making a decision. Pause to take a break. Pause to determine what I need. Pause to remind myself that what people do and say defines them and not me. Pause everywhere. The sense that everything is urgent and that I don't have time to pause is a lie. Actually, pausing invariably saves time.

Love. I need to care for me as I would for a child I love. Are you hungry? Do you need a snack? Should I put you down for a nap? Are you feeling cooped up? Let's go for a long walk. What do you need? What do you really need? I will find it for you. I am here for you. I see you. I hear you. I believe you. I believe in you.

Misconceptions Around Self-Care

The belief that self-care or self-love is "selfish".

The sense that self-care is complicated or time consuming. Self-care can be a glass of water.

The assumption that boundaries make you difficult or rigid.

The notion that being clear on what you should expect from others means you are picky or challenging.

Feeling like wanting makes you demanding or unreasonable.

The sense that having needs makes you a burden or too much.

That any form of self-care, such as resting, giving yourself time, giving yourself space, is something you have to earn or deserve.

That self-care is only for women.

That self-care is whatever feels good. Things that are harmful to your long-term health are not self-care, even if they feel a treat.

That self-care is expensive. Making a difficult decision, taking a nap or taking a social media break are free.

That loving yourself implies a choice and that you are sacrificing anyone who loves you to put yourself first. (You are in fact putting yourself in a place where you can give the best of you to others, rather than a resentful, bitter, drained you.)

Things I've Stopped Doing

Things I've stopped doing:

I've stopped scrolling. If I catch myself mindlessly scrolling through social media, I put the phone down and turn my attention to something more valuable (or at least more mindful).

I like to stay informed but I no longer constantly look at the news.

I've stopped drinking. I was never much of a drinker but realized drinking made me tired and fuzzy so now I don't drink at all. Sparkling water is just as festive as champagne.

Things I'm practicing doing less of:

Worrying.

Feeling like I always have to be busy.

Feeling like I have to fix things for other people.

Overthinking.

Suffering over things that have only taken place in my imagination.

Eating past the point of comfort.

Feeling like I have to convince others to like or love me.

Feeling like I need to be right.

Feeling like I need to be in control.

Saying yes when I should be saying no.

Beliefs That Hurt Us

Everyone has it all together except for me.

A bad relationship is better than being alone.

I can change another.

I can convince someone to love me.

Control makes me strong.

Approval is a priority.

Getting everything perfect is what makes me worthy.

Practice makes perfect.

Saying yes to everything proves my loyalty and commitment.

If someone does not do things my way they are doing it wrong.

I need another to make me happy.

Others should know what I need.

I am supposed to be happy all the time.

I am valuable only if I am productive.

A roller coaster of emotions equals passion.

Stability is boring.

Boundaries are a form of rejection.

True love does not require boundaries.

If you love me you shouldn't need space.

The only thing that matters is intent.

Having needs means I'm needy.

Familiar means good.

Relationships are supposed to be forever.

Forgiving means things go on as if what hurt me had never happened.

White lies are OK because they are designed to protect you.

Taking care of myself means I am selfish.

What Holds Us Back?

I will get everything perfect.

I will control everything.

I will say yes to everything and leave myself open to feeling exhausted and taken advantage of.

I will determine boundaries are selfish and as such will have none.

I will decide saying no means I am not loyal or dedicated enough.

I believe I am not good enough and this belief will influence all my decisions.

I believe I am helpless and cannot do things without others doing them for me.

I will live with envy in my heart for all the things others can have that I can't have.

I will be perpetually attracted to people who are not available to me or don't treat me well.

I am afraid that others will judge me so I will take no risks.

I will be angry at anyone who does not see things the way I see them.

I will commit to things and then not follow through so I can show me I cannot really be counted on.

I will make excuses to justify things I do that are not good for me. (I've had a rough week and deserve this plate of french fries.)

I think people who truly love me should just know what I want so instead of spelling it out I will get angry if they don't get it right.

I will never ask for help.

I will live convinced that I don't deserve good things, and don't deserve to be loved.

How Can I Understand Our World?

Don't believe anything you think and consider the following principles:

Things seldom happen for just one reason.

If you cannot separate yourself from your thoughts, you can't know what you don't know.

When objects interact, they can form a system with a quality the isolated objects don't have (such as neurons creating consciousness).

The most adopted philosophies were built to be easily believed rather than built to be true.

Mistakes grow because one belief is built on another.

We think the world is as we see it, but there is more that we can't see. For example, we only understand killers through the ones that got caught.

A trend can appear in a group of data and disappear when groups are combined. This means that even the strongest correlations can be a fallacy.

Whatever it is you are worried or obsessing about seems more important than everything else, just because you're thinking about it.

As a social issue improves, how we define it expands giving us the illusion that it's getting worse.

People don't get their information from where it is but from where it's easier to see.

We judge the strength of an argument by how appealing we find the conclusion.

A group can go along with something no one likes due to believing others approve.

People often reject a philosophy by comparing it to another that is impossible to attain.

Words that mean the same can give you a completely different impression of what you are describing.

An excess of anything can cause a rise in the opposite.

When you see something good in a person you assume other good things.

We view groups of people as homogenous.

Advantage begets advantage.

People are promoted to their level of incompetence, then get stuck.

We describe something as undefinable when we cannot defend it.

Every one of these is a principle, and there are many more that shed light on all the things we cannot help perceive as they are not.

How Can I Live the Life I Want?

Spend time alone so you can get to know yourself. It's the only way to distinguish how you see you from how others see you. How others see you does not define you, even if it will often feel like it does.

Spend time alone so you can hear yourself. It's the only way to identify what you really want.

Once you know what you want, break it down into small steps and do something to move towards what you want every day. Always be clear on what you are working towards.

Once you know what you want, learn to ask for it.

Stop convincing others to love you, stop pretending, stop people pleasing, stop doing things you don't really want to do, stop prioritizing "being polite" over standing up for yourself and stop lying.

Set boundaries. Defend them. Stay away from people who do not respect them. Nurture relationships with people who do.

Speaking of relationships, they matter so much. They are worth the work it takes to figure them out. It's so tempting to give up on them. Don't.

Get comfortable with our constant companions: loneliness, doubt, uneasiness, change and uncertainty.

Learn all about cognitive distortions. Knowing them will help you think more clearly. It will help you not believe what you think. It will help you witness your thoughts instead of just thinking them.

Learn to recognize your ego.

Keep things simple. Own less. Do less. Travel light.

Learn what it means to live "in the now." "Some day" never comes.

Learn something new every day.

Encourage and inspire others.

Take good care of yourself. Love yourself. Don't listen to anyone who tells you this is selfish. You're all you've got.

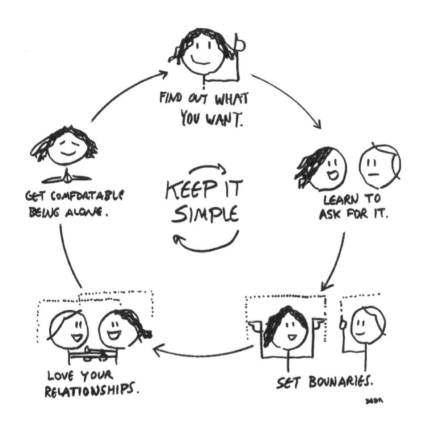

FIND OUT WHAT YOU WANT.

GET COMFORTABLE BEING ALONE.

KEEP IT SIMPLE

LEARN TO ASK FOR IT.

LOVE YOUR RELATIONSHIPS.

SET BOUNARIES.

Examples of Platitudes

Find your purpose.

Your soulmate is out there, waiting for you.

It will happen if it was meant to be.

True love is unconditional.

Love conquers all.

Everything happens for a reason.

Good things come to those who wait.

Other people have it much worse than you.

What doesn't kill you makes you stronger.

All you need is a positive attitude.

Think outside the box.

He is in a much better place now.

Age is just a number.

Never, ever give up.

179

Must-Haves

Hunger.

Restlessness.

A tendency towards exhausting yourself.

Discontent.

Courage.

Receptivity.

Curiosity.

A sense of adventure.

A natural inclination towards experimenting.

A clear — but not too clear — grasp on your own fallibility and your own mortality.

A resistance to routine, no matter how tempting routine can be.

A minor allergic reaction to what is familiar.

A sense of wonder.

An eye for beauty.

An ability to listen.

Self-awareness. (You know what? Get two.)

A gravitational pull towards discomfort.

Awe.

A knack for inviting serendipity.

A sense of peace, even if it's fleeting. Just enough to grant you the ability to leave the future for later, which is where it belongs.

Things I've Grown To Accept

I don't have to wait to get everything perfect to love myself. I can go ahead and do that right now.

Everyone has disagreements, makes mistakes, experiences loss and doubt and struggles. Imperfection is pervasive, rampant, unrestrained and exuberant.

Expressing my limits is not disloyal, and looking out for my needs is not selfish.

Accepting more means struggling less. Plus, no amount of struggle will alter the truth I believe I can resist. Truth doesn't care that it's being resisted.

I was never supposed to be anyone other than who I am.

I never need to apologize for wanting something different.

No one is meant to fill my needs. They are meant to fill their own.

People cannot love me the way I want them to. They can only love me the way they love.

Change is meant to be embraced and celebrated. I mean, I can reject and shun it but it's going to happen anyway so I might as well throw it a party.

The more responsibility I am willing to take the more powerful I become.

Attempting to change another person is self-destructive.

A busy schedule is overrated.

Procrastination is resistance.

Unpredictability is overrated.

Surrender is underrated.

Curiosity is underrated.

Learning to pause is underrated.

Crying is underrated.

Control is overrated. Also, it doesn't exist.

If any relationship demands that I prove myself, it's not worth it.

Emotions are easier to understand if I accept them as contradictory. For example, grief and relief.

It's never a good idea to leave saying "I love you" for later.

Even if I have no idea how to get something that I want, I can begin by making space for it.

Lists About Relationships

Ways To Say No

No.

No, thank you.

I don't want to.

I can't do ___, but I am happy to do ___.

I can't do that right now.

I am already overcommitted.

I won't be able to.

I have too much on my plate.

That sounds like fun but I won't make it.

I can't be there but thank you for thinking of me!

I am not a fan of ___ so I'll pass.

This day/week/month/year has been hard and I need a time out.

What "Nice" Behavior
Is Actually Toxic?

I will have no boundaries.

I will not recognize your boundaries.

I will ignore what I need to focus on what you need.

I put you first and consider not doing so a form of betrayal.

I will ignore, deny, diminish or allow hurtful and unacceptable things.

I will give you unwanted, unsolicited "constructive criticism".

I will make excuses for you.

I will justify what you do.

I will lie for you.

I will cover up for you.

I will take the blame for you.

I will take responsibility for what is your responsibility.

I will run interference for you in your relationships.

I will take all your problems as if they were mine and worry, research, help and solve them for you.

TRY THIS!

What Makes a Person Defensive?

I perceive you as a threat.

I perceive something about you as a threat.

You have power over me.

I feel attacked.

I feel diminished.

I feel criticized.

I feel I am being treated unfairly.

I feel I am at a disadvantage.

I have a lot to lose.

I feel unheard.

I feel overlooked.

I feel triggered as I have a history of feeling unsafe.

I am not good at communicating.

I don't know how to assert myself.

I feel weak.

I feel guilty.

I feel ashamed.

I am hiding something.

Before this even started I was already feeling like I didn't belong.

How To Ruin a Great Relationship

Enforce a zero tolerance policy on mistakes. Make certain you get this relationship perfect.

Blame any shortcomings on the other to ensure your record remains clean.

Overthink and overanalyze in an effort to not mess it up.

Control everything.

Expect the other person to play a role in managing your emotions. If you feel jealous or possessive, limit what she does and who she sees. If you feel separation anxiety, cling.

Give up your life, your friends and your interests and place it all on the shoulders of this new relationship.

Forget about boundaries. Yours and his.

Make sure you never voice your expectations, concerns or feelings so that the other person has to walk blindfolded across your inner landscape.

Filter what you hear through what you feel insecure about so that your understanding of things is corrupted by the reasons you believe you are not good enough.

Assume the other person is out to get you. Act accordingly.

Use charm, white lies and an arsenal of special effects to avoid arguments.

You can dodge how you feel when you are alone by spending all your time with the other person.

When you are with the other person, let everything distract you. A passing thought, your phone, the email you have to send. You have so much to do.

Remain firmly anchored to the past. Bonus points if you remain firmly anchored to a past relationship.

Turn small things into big things. The faster they escalate the better.

Pay attention to anything you are afraid of and prioritize it over hope, over faith and over love. Prioritize it over what is actually taking place.

Talk a lot about your unwillingness to allow anything or anyone to change you.

The Difference Between Excusing and Understanding

Understanding is a miraculous, life-affirming, healing mixture of comprehension, empathy and compassion. It makes me more lenient, more tolerant, more receptive, kinder; but it does not compromise my limits, my safety or my sense of dignity.

How you can tell you are excusing someone's behavior:

An absence of boundaries. Boundaries would sound like *"I understand you have been through a terrible time, but this does not mean you can treat me poorly."*

Noticing that I am making another person's behavior my responsibility. For example, feeling that I am walking on eggshells to avoid "provoking" the behavior that hurts me.

In my mind I diminish the events that caused me pain. *"That wasn't so bad"* or *"she is so very busy at work"* or *"he is a very sensitive person"* or *"I don't want to add to her considerable burden."* This is not generous. This is me messing with my own perception.

An inability to communicate. I cannot explain how I feel without risking an outburst so I skip the explanation. This results in me forgiving or brushing aside unacceptable behavior that has never been discussed or acknowledged.

196

I become an enabler. I spend a lot of time explaining to others why she is behaving the way she is. This means that through my explaining I separate her from the consequences of her actions.

I see what you could be, what this relationship could be, if only. Relationships are not "potential." Relationships are not somewhere in the future when circumstances become ideal. Relationships are now.

UNDERSTANDING
HIS BEHAVIOR

EXCUSING HIS
BEHAVIOR

Unrealistic Expectations

Bewitching love at first sight.

Glancing at someone across a crowded room and hearing violins.

The enchanted arrival of our soulmate.

A person who will be our everything.

A person who will belong to us.

A person who will make us dazzlingly happy.

A person who will deliver us from feeling lost or purposeless.

A person who will read our mind, rendering communication obsolete.

That this person will complete us.

That we don't need boundaries, as we are one.

That we will agree on everything.

That this person will change to accommodate us.

That every day will be new, exciting and filled with passion.

Sex every day that feels orgasmic, enrapturing, spellbinding.

That we will not have eyes for anyone else.

That the relationship will last forever.

That we will live happily ever after.

That we will ride off straight into the sunset on perfectly cared for horses.

Codependent

I know I am in a codependent relationship if:

How you feel about me is the measure of my worth. If you don't love me I am worth nothing.

Your feelings are my responsibility.

I would do anything to avoid a fight.

I can't say no or express any boundary because it feels too much like it would risk our relationship.

I am so worried about the fact you might feel unhappy that I never stop to consider how I feel.

I find it very difficult to make my own decisions.

I don't know who I am.

I don't know what I want.

I have no interests outside of you.

I am so focused on what you or others say about me that I don't really know how I feel about me.

I set anything I think or want aside to make room for what you think or want.

Healthy love is more of who I am: a better me, a more confident me, a me full of self-expression. Codependency is me, lost in you.

I WILL DO ANYTHING FOR YOU. FOREVER.

CODEPENDENCE.

When To Break Up

Most of our relationship is work.

Spending time with you is exhausting.

I find myself walking on eggshells to avoid a fight instead having the will to talk through our differences.

When we do talk I feel I'm always wrong.

I am constantly asking myself how to decide if I need to leave and I mostly stay because I'm afraid to make the wrong decision.

I don't trust you.

Either one of us has broken the terms of our relationship.

I can barely remember the last time I felt happy instead of drained.

Our personalities are incompatible.

We fundamentally want different things that cannot be reconciled.

Early Signs of Incompatibility

You want to commit and I don't want commitment.

I need alone time and you need my company.

I need space and you want us to live together.

I don't want to get married and you do.

I don't want kids and you do.

You want me to love only you and I love you but love other people too.

I like saving and you like spending.

What you think is funny I think is cruel.

Your bedtime is my "up and at them!" time.

We define "frequent sex" differently.

I think I'm an optimist and you think I'm naive.

You want involvement and to me it feels like control.

I crave intimacy and intimacy makes you uncomfortable.

I think love is change and you refuse to let anything change you.

We believe different things.

We want different things.

You voted for Trump.

Healthy Relationship

We trust each other.

We assume the best of one another.

We feel at peace, both with and away from each other.

Sex is a priority and is broadly defined, not just intercourse.

We talk about the life we want for ourselves and it involves
the other.

We conduct ourselves with compassion, towards each other and
towards ourselves.

We feel safe.

We don't blame.

We respect ourselves and each other.

We have clear boundaries.

We encourage time alone.

We do not punish each other.

We take responsibility for our own actions.

We work on ourselves.

We see ourselves and each other as flawed.

We know what we want.

We can see each other's point, even when we disagree.

We don't conclude the other is wrong when they are not like us.

We know that if there are two of us, there are two realities that are equally real.

We understand we are not each other's "everything".

We know how not to take things personally.

We are aware of our own expectations.

Difficult conversations may be stressful but they are not scary.

If we want different things and one of us says "no" there is no drama, no guilt, no manipulation, no putting the other down, even in the presence of disappointment.

We use communication — words — instead of assumptions, attempting to interpret what the other meant, or expecting anyone to guess or put things together.

When we fight we fight well, then work towards mending the aftermath.

We are able to say things that put us in a vulnerable position.

We create our own traditions and rituals.

We support each other without taking on what the other is feeling.

We don't try to control each other.

We laugh.

We see each other as allies.

We believe in each other.

We are so happy to see the other do well.

We want what's best for one another.

How Can I Stop Being Codependent?

You are not one. You are two.

Spend time alone — afternoons, days, weekends — even if it runs counter to what you want to do. Make spending time alone something that brings you joy, rather than something you have to endure. This might take practice.

When alone, listen to yourself. It's the time you gain an understanding over what you want.

Communicate what you prefer, what you want, what you need.

Learn as much as you can about setting boundaries and saying no. You don't say no even if you are deeply in love. You say no because you are deeply in love and are cultivating a healthy relationship.

Remember that feeling resentment is an inner message that you have compromised yourself. It's a sign that says *"we need a boundary right here."*

Spend time pursuing things that interest you, that contribute to you having a part of your life that is your own. They can be social (a book club, running buddies, a swim team) or individual (reading, writing, photography).

Do things just for you.

Separate "me" from "you" and from "us." Develop an awareness for every time either of you speak as if your opinions were all the same. *"We love coffee." "We hated that movie!"*

Understand you are not responsible for the emotions of others, and no one is responsible for yours.

Learn that you are lovable and do not need to do anything to "earn" someone's love.

Every day, practice loving yourself, which for the most part involves the things mentioned above.

Reasons Not To Assume

You don't know anything about how another person feels. ("*Wow. This guy looks like he's mad at me.*")

You fill in what you don't know with your own interpretation. ("*It must have been something I said.*")

Your interpretation is not based on the other person, but in you. Mostly your insecurities and your experiences. ("*He probably hates me.*")

You begin making conclusions based on information that does not actually exist. ("*It's so common for people to hate me for no reason.*")

In this way it's impossible to reach an accurate conclusion. ("*Why does everybody hate me?*")

You begin to live inside the stories that you fabricate, rather than in the real world. ("*Why doesn't anybody understand me?*")

You never learn to do things that are hard but necessary, such as ask, talk, clarify, confirm.

Examples of Passive-Aggressive Behavior

If instead of expressing a feeling clearly and directly I resort to expressing it indirectly, that is called being passive-aggressive.

This might be pouting or acting sullen or moody.

Eye rolling.

Gossiping to someone else about what you do, instead of talking to you.

Deliberately leaving for later what you really need me to do.

Forgetting things you keep asking me to do.

Sarcasm. I say things that border on mean, but make them sound like I'm just being funny. (*"Oh, come on! Don't be so sensitive!"*)

I moan about small things all day but fail to address what is really bothering me.

I agree to do something I don't want to do, and then never show up on time.

Instead of *"what you said hurt my feelings"* I give you the silent treatment.

I make plans with our group of friends but don't invite you.

Instead of stating something clearly I disguise it as a joke. I might then say *"I was kidding! I think you are exaggerating."*

Any insult disguised as a compliment: *"This document is a really good start!"*

Instead of saying *"our relationship feels distant"* I begin to cancel plans at the last minute or fail to show up when I said I would.

Passive-aggressive people are not evil. They are usually attempting to do something about how they feel despite feeling they cannot do it head on.

Being passive-aggressive is not very effective. It lacks clarity and as such does not typically result in resolving whatever is bothering me.

How To Support Loved Ones

I resist the urge to say anything that denies, disrespects or diminishes anyone's experience, such as:

"Calm down!"

"Suck it up!"

"Keep it together!"

"Be strong!"

"Don't be so sensitive!"

"Let it go!"

"Try not to think about it."

"It's really not that bad."

"This is nothing."

"It could be so much worse."

"Everything happens for a reason!"

"Why don't you...." (or any attempt to save, fix, improve, rescue).

Instead, I try:

"You are such a good friend to me. I want to be a good friend to you."

"What can I do that would make you feel supported?"

"I would love to just listen."

"I am so sorry."

"That sounds awful/difficult/complex."

"It makes sense for you to feel sad/upset/angry."

"You inspire me."

"I am proud of you."

"You did not deserve this."

"This is not your fault."

"I understand."

"I trust you."

"I believe you."

Then, some things I try to do:

Stay close.

Check in.

Give them space. (This is a balance based on me asking how I can support them.)

Help out with specific, pre-agreed upon things (such as running errands for them, bringing food over, etc.).

How To Break Your Own Heart

If I wanted to break my own heart, I would long for things but never speak of them. I would expect people around me to guess, as a way to measure their interest and the level of their attention.

I would let my expectations run unchecked, rampant, and wait for others to act like I anticipated.

I would meet someone and make plans to change him.

I would meet someone who treated others poorly, convinced things would be different with me.

I would meet someone, decide he is my soulmate and make him my everything. He'd fulfill my every need.

I would set no boundaries. I would not be needing them.

This man would save me and be forever responsible for my happiness. Look at him. The answer to every one of my big life questions.

This is what I would do, if what I wanted was to break my own heart.

Why Losing a Friend Feels Like a Breakup

Because, wasn't this supposed to be forever?

Because I feel betrayed.

Because I feel wronged.

Because I've lost someone important.

Because, when will I see you again?

Because, when will we talk again?

Because my life was a certain shape, and now that shape has changed.

Because at one point we chose each other.

Because I don't know exactly what happened.

Because I am tired of analyzing this.

Because I feel I did everything wrong.

Because I feel I never really knew you.

Because if something was bothering you, you never bothered to tell me.

Because you didn't think this was worth untangling.

Because on top of it all, what I feel is shame.

Because I question myself and my worth.

Because a breakup is more clean-cut than this.

Things To Look For in a Date

A lack of interest in fairy tales. I mean, even the shoes sound really uncomfortable.

That both parties be clear on what they want and what they need, can express it and stand up for it.

An ability to both articulate and respect boundaries.

Clear communication, including a willingness to have difficult conversations.

Trust, in every direction.

A healthy, ever-evolving relationship with themselves.

An ability to assume the best in each other.

Follow through, reliability, predictability.

A desire for intimacy.

A desire for evolution.

A desire.

A symmetry between effort and ease.

A natural, fundamental compatibility.

A shared sense of wonder.

218

How To Be Respected

Become aware of every time you are doing something to please another, get approval or validation or get someone to like you, and instead strive to be happy with yourself.

Set boundaries and learn everything about them. Make peace with the fact you will never get them exactly right and keep trying anyway.

If you think or feel anything, honor it, instead of believing you can't, shouldn't, that "it doesn't make sense" or that it proves there is something wrong with you.

Speak up.

Advocate for yourself and what you need.

Make your well being a priority.

Invest in relationships where you are appreciated. Disinvest in relationships where you are not.

Define yourself, rather than feeling like the opinions or behaviors of others dictate who you are or how you are doing.

Develop self-compassion.

Refuse to settle.

Identify what you are good at and give it breath, time, space, life. Place what you create at the center of your swirling life.

What I'm trying to tell you is this: The only way to "make others respect you" is to respect yourself.

The only way to
"make others respect
you" is to respect yourself.

MY OWN
SELF-RESPECT.

I respect
me!

OTHER PEOPLE'S.
RESPECT OF ME.

R E S P E C T

bzar

Signs That Someone Respects You

There is a natural tuning in to each other — a strong level of attention, of presence.

By "natural" I mean I don't have to constantly demand it.

Everything is tinged with a fundamental kindness — not just in how we treat each other but in how we treat those around us.

We are considerate of each other.

There is a sense of inclusion.

We believe in each other.

We observe each other's boundaries.

If something is not clear, we ask. Assuming that I know without asking infringes on your preferences.

If I expect something I state it. Expecting you to guess is not reasonable.

We listen to each other.

We talk through things together.

We do what we say we are going to do. Follow through is a display of respect, for others but also for myself.

We tell the truth, even when it's hard.

We feel safe, even when we disagree.

We feel safe, even when our opinions or beliefs are different.

We feel safe, even when we mess something up.

We hold difficult conversations.

We trust each other.

We value and are grateful for the other person — the opposite of taking each other for granted. Gratitude is respect in the most elegant attire.

If something isn't right, we talk about it.

If we fight, the intent is to understand, not to win. Being deliberately hurtful is the absence of respect.

There is accountability — an ease in saying *"That was me. I am responsible."*

Dealbreakers

Feeling like I'm not safe.

Any form of abuse: violence, of course, but also gaslighting, putting me down, yelling, attempts to control me or manage reality.

Evidence of cruelty.

An absence of trust.

An inability to rely on the other person.

Lies/attempts to deceive.

If the relationship needs to be a secret, for any reason.

We want different things (he wants kids, I don't) or have serious issues with a lack of compatibility (related to lifestyle, sex, money, outlook, values). This leaves both of us perpetually feeling like we can't ever get anything right.

Indifference.

Emotional Intimacy

Emotional intimacy is not:

Urgent.

Desperate.

One-sided.

Secret spilling.

Emotional dumping.

Instant.

Forced.

Codependent.

Emotional intimacy is:

Balanced, harmonious, reciprocal. It expresses itself with ease.

We are invested in each other.

We can really talk.

We can share things we might not normally share: both dreams and fears.

We can sit in silence.

I trust you, you trust me.

We feel safe.

We can be who we are.

I feel you see me. You feel I see you.

We feel heard.

I feel you understand me. You too feel understood.

I feel you accept me. You feel I accept you.

You don't think I am perfect and like me anyway. I like you and don't think you're perfect either.

We respect each other.

We support each other.

We accomplish things together.

We solve things together.

We can be apart and still feel connected.

We recognize and respect each other's boundaries.

We understand it takes time.

It can be broken and repaired.

How To Recover From a Breakup

For the first couple of weeks after a breakup I have one task: to hold on. That's it. I remind myself that feelings are temporary, that one day I will not feel this way anymore.

Then, I tell myself that what happened is not related to my self-worth. I am worth loving and what I am going through right now does not indicate that I am not.

I identify what I miss. Sure, I miss him. But also a lot of what I lost is the part of me he brought out. Who was she, this person that I was? How can I keep her here?

I set aside skepticism, doubt and any thought that might hurt me. Was what we had ever real? Did he ever love me? Was this all a lie? I don't need to play mind games with myself. I am in enough pain.

I refrain from "finding out" anything. No scrolling through social media. No talking to common friends. No attempts to run into him.

I reject anything that will keep me tied to feeling like this, which includes fantasies about revenge. I want to move on.

I exercise. The very last thing I want is to move. I do it anyway.

I stay in the present. Right here with me is where it's at.

I throw out any negative talk. You are terrible at relationships. Actually, fights are normal. Breakups are normal. Relationship longevity is not relationship success.

I surround myself with love. I spend time with my family and friends. I double down on learning to love myself. Self-love is the antidote.

I get someone to touch me. I ask my friends to hug me. I go get a massage. For me, touch deprivation is a thing, and being touched is healing.

I get out of my head. I call friends and talk about them. I help out others. I forget about me for a while.

I make a list of things I neglected in order to make room for my relationship. I love to read and now I have time. I love to spend the day alone and wander. I love poetry readings and swimming. I love rock climbing and learning new things.

I make a list of things I have always wanted to do. I have never been to New Zealand. I want to see the Northern Lights. I want to learn how to make macarons. Or maybe I just want to go to a macaron making class so I can meet other people interested in making macarons.

I remind myself that love is a privilege. That I want to love well. That the only way to love well is to practice, and get my heart broken, and recover, and try again.

(11) GET SOMEONE TO TOUCH ME.

(12) GET OUT OF MY HEAD.

(13) LIST THE THINGS I NEGLECTED.

(14) LIST THE THINGS I WANT TO DO.

(15) REMEMBER LOVE IS A PRIVILEGE.

RECOVER + TRY AGAIN.

(10) SURROUND MYSELF WITH LOVE.

(9) THROW OUT ANY NEGATIVE TALK.

(8) STAY IN THE PRESENT.

(7) EXERCISE.

(6) REJECT REVENGE

(1) HOLD ON

(2) KNOW THAT I'M WORTH LOVING

(3) IDENTIFY WHAT I MISS.

(4) SET ASIDE SKEPTICISM.

(5) REFRAIN FROM "FINDING OUT."

TREATMENT FOR A BREAKUP.

START HERE

229

These Things Are Normal

Instead of believing what I see in movies, fairy tales and social media, it helps me to remember that:

Fear — of being vulnerable, of being exposed, and fear that I'm going to screw this up — is universal.

I am most definitely going to screw this up because screwing things up is what we do.

Regarding the other as flawed is better — and more accurate — than believing he is perfect.

Fighting and disagreeing is typical.

Awkward is typical.

Difficult is typical.

Feeling that we are different — rather than feeling that we are one — is good.

Feeling a love, an intimacy and a sexual desire that is fluctuating rather than static or steady is normal.

Feeling it's hard to make time for a relationship is natural.

Navigating change — in him, in me, in circumstances — is inevitable.

Bungling up communication is what happens to even professional communicators.

Being really clumsy in setting and respecting boundaries is part of basic relationship negotiation. No one "gets it right." Not even people who write books about boundaries.

Feeling unsure — about me, about us, about life — is natural.

Feeling attraction towards others is healthy.

Being in a relationship and sometimes longing to be single is commonplace, as is being single and longing to be in a relationship. Humans are creatures of longing.

Counting on other people — friends, coworkers — to meet some of our needs is good. Our significant others are not "everything".

Finally — and this is my favorite because the better I understand it the less I suffer — many, many things that happen in my relationship are not about me. Someone needing time away from me — time with his friends, or time for himself — is healthy and not related to me or his feelings for me or our relationship.

Don't Be Sorry for These

I am sorry for setting boundaries.

I am sorry for my feelings.

I am sorry I have a question or need something clarified.

I am sorry that I don't know.

I am sorry I can't attend your party.

I am sorry I did not get back to you as quickly as you wanted me to.

I am sorry that I am busy.

I am sorry I am not drinking.

I am sorry I am ordering the salad and a side of vegetables.

I am sorry that I need time alone.

I am sorry that I am not feeling well.

I am sorry, but no.

I am sorry I want something other than what you want.

I am sorry I need more affection.

I am sorry I need more attention.

I am sorry that I am doing well.

I am sorry we disagree.

I am sorry I have my own opinion.

I am sorry I have an opinion that's different from the opinion I used to have.

I am sorry for being who I am and not who you want or expect me to be.

Difference Between 'Care' and 'Control'

Control is any attempt to influence another person's behavior. By "any attempt" I mean any attempt, even if the attempt is "for their own good".

Control is *"I don't think you should hang out with __ "* or any form of criticism even if it's disguised as "helpful" or "constructive".

Control is any form of approval that seems conditional: you do what I want, in exchange for which I will love you.

Control means making me feel like I need to earn being treated well. Control is belittling, saying things that make me doubt myself.

Control is anything that feels like the other person is keeping score, making me feel pressured, guilty, indebted, beholden or unworthy.

Control is an invasion of privacy: surveillance, snooping.

Control is making me responsible for his feelings. *"You can't see guy friends, it makes me jealous."*

234

Control is an inability to accept I have other things in my life going on besides him — even the refusal to understand the importance of time alone.

Care is simple. I see you. I hear you. I accept you. I support you. I grant you space to be, do, feel. I love you because you are you, in exchange for which I need nothing.

It's Codependent

If I want to change, improve, fix or save someone, "for their own good", if I want to "help", it's not generosity. It's codependency.

Neglecting to get to know, identify and express my limits is not selfless. It's codependent.

The tendency to want to keep someone else's secrets is not a display of trust. It's codependent.

Distorting what I want or what I need to keep the peace is not dedication. It's codependent.

The inability to distinguish your emotions from mine is not intimacy. It's codependent.

Codependency is pervasive and infiltrates all our relationships because we confuse it with love.

We confuse it with love and then we wonder why love hurts so much, why it leaves us resentful and empty.

Examples of Vulnerability

I am sorry.

I need help.

I feel lost.

I am struggling.

I feel inadequate.

I feel powerless.

I feel small.

I am hurting.

I am lonely.

I am sad.

I don't know.

I can't.

I made a mistake.

I was wrong.

I am afraid.

People To Stay Away From

People who diminish me.

People who disregard or disrespect my boundaries.

People who deny my reality or my experience or don't make room for the possibility that a different version can be just as true.

People who deny my feelings. *"Don't be so sensitive!"*

People who make me feel like I'm not safe.

People who take my energy rather than leaving me feeling recharged and inspired.

People who are not happy if I do well.

Anyone who tries to isolate me from family or friends.

Anyone who places expectations on me and expects me to be that.

Any dynamic that lacks balance. I feel like I am always the one who __.

Any form of contempt: being belittled, made fun of, being made to feel inadequate.

Anyone I find myself making excuses for.

Any form of cruelty towards anyone.

And, most importantly, am I the one inadvertently displaying any of these behaviors, towards myself or towards others?

I work on making sure I'm on my side, because there is no staying away from me.

It's a One-Sided Relationship If —

You and I both are extremely interested in you.

I do the calling, the coordinating, the planning, the accommodating. You do the last minute changing or canceling.

After we spend time together I feel empty.

After we spend time together I have a sick feeling that I've been taken advantage of.

I feel like my feelings and my efforts and my enthusiasm spill all over everything so I am constantly apologizing for me.

You are hurtful and instead of recognizing that you are hurtful I justify your behavior. You did after all have a very long day, and I can be so annoying.

I can't count on you. I mean, because you are always so busy. You do have a lot on your plate.

I fret all the time that I have offended or irritated you, that I am falling short, or that you will leave me.

When you think of the future you think of you. When I think of the future I think of us.

You spend most of your time on you, your projects, your goals; and I spend most of my time on you, your projects, your goals.

Alas. Neither you nor I have time for me.

Is Being Child-Free Selfish?

If you choose to have children, that's awesome.

If you choose to not have children, that's awesome.

What is selfish is to judge the choices another person makes.

The only person with the authority on someone's life choices is the person living that life.

In the case of your life, that is only you.

In the case of mine, that is only me.

Why It's Better Not To Lie

Every time I lie I know I lied. Lies teach me that I cannot be trusted.

Lies force me to be someone I am not, and tell me that who I am needs faking.

Every time I lie I will have to lie to cover the lie. The effect of a lie is exponential lying.

If you sense that something is wrong and someone lies to you "so you don't worry" you speculate and probably imagine things are worse than they are. No one should be left at the mercy of their imagination.

If you know something isn't in its place and you are lied to you have to choose between trusting the liar or trusting yourself. This choice is particularly terrible for kids: they tend to choose trusting what adults say over trusting themselves. This is how they learn not to trust their own internal navigating tools.

If I lie to you for any reason I believe is worthy of a lie, I will break your trust. Trust is really difficult to repair.

If I lie to you I am teaching you to lie to me. I am establishing it as acceptable behavior in the dynamics of our relationship.

If I lie to you I am telling you that you are not worth a difficult conversation. Lies make the person being lied to feel like they don't matter.

Honest communication and difficult conversations make relationships stronger. Lies make them weaker.

If there are difficulties I am not sharing with you, I am allowing you to be surprised. Why not share things from the beginning, when dealing with difficult things will make us resilient?

Lies and secrets make everyone — including the liar and secret keeper — feel isolated, alone and disconnected. Connection is what humans thrive on.

Compliments That Are Not About Looks

"Life feels lighter with you."

"Life feels new with you, fresh with you."

"With you, colors seem hyper-saturated."

"I learn so much from you."

"I love the way you see."

"I love the way you think. I admire your intelligence, your viewpoint, your work ethic. I love that you change my mind, grant me a new perspective, and make me think."

"I love that you are thoughtful. It makes me want to be more thoughtful."

"I love how you always put effort into what you do, your best foot forward, how you want to do things well."

"I feel safe with you. Comfortable with you. Understood with you. Heard by you. Seen by you. Important with you."

"I don't feel judged by you."

"I can be myself with you."

"I want to be better because of you."

"I feel young when I am with you."

"I like how you take responsibility. Your confidence. Your honesty."

"I like how you break things down to make them easier
to understand."

"It's splendid to watch how you make hard things seem easy."

"I really like to see how you treat others, how you interact with
others, how you react to others."

"It's so sexy, how you listen. How you're curious. How
you're caring."

"You are such a good friend. A good ally. A good partner. I feel
you're on my side."

"I feel less alone with you."

What Is It Like To Feel Safe?

I feel accepted — loved— for who I already am. I don't need to make an effort to deliver what is expected of me.

I feel understood.

I feel respected. I know I will not be diminished or made fun of.

I know what to expect.

I never feel I have to walk on eggshells.

I feel like you do what you say you are going to do.

I know you tell me the truth.

I know you have nothing to hide.

I know there is no part of me I need to hide.

I know we can disagree without me feeling threatened.

I know I can say no and not feel like I'm putting us at risk.

I know I can say no and you will know it's not a form of rejection.

I am not trapped in an involuntary system of reward and punishment.

There are no outbursts or reactions that make me feel I am standing on something precarious.

I know we can talk, either to share something or to talk our way through anything.

This sense of safety is not a luxury. It's the least we can ask for in any kind of relationship. Without it, our growth and ability to evolve are stunted because we are too busy burning our life force on trying to survive.

Relationship Traps

I think he's perfect.

I think he can save me.

He can complete me.

I can change him.

I can fix him.

He is all I need.

He defines me.

His feelings for me are the measure of my worth.

He belongs to me.

If he's jealous that means he loves me.

He should be able to guess what I want.

He should be able to know why I'm not happy.

I won't express what I want or need until I'm sure he likes me.

I will avoid disagreeing so he doesn't leave me.

Boundaries are selfish.

True love means boundaries are unnecessary.

We are one.

Happily ever after.

Reasons Why Some People Don't Have Friends

It is extremely common for people to have no friends. Here are a few reasons why:

Because their lives are full and making friends does not seem possible.

Because their lives are full and making friends is not a priority.

Because they are 100% busy with something — such as keeping their job or caring for their family or caring for someone who is sick — and have no time left for anything else.

Because they are loners.

Because they are massively introverted and social interaction is too overwhelming.

Because they have been hurt and would rather be alone than get hurt again.

Because they have social anxiety and interacting feels unsurmountable.

Because they are extremely shy and don't know how not to be.

Because they are interested in different things and haven't found people like them.

Because they are experiencing something big — grief, depression — that leaves no space for anything else.

Because they want friends but have a blind spot regarding what they do that keeps people away, for example, they are (intentionally or not) hurtful, pushy, demanding, controlling, unreasonable.

Because of where their life is at. They've had friends in the past but now they are in a new town, or just switched jobs, or just got a divorce — and suddenly their situation requires that they start over.

Because of where their life is at. They've had friends in the past and it used to be easy but now everyone is wrapped up in whatever and how does one make friends as an adult?

Worst Relationship Advice

Your soulmate is out there!

You are too picky.

He should make the first move.

Play hard to get.

Remain a mystery.

Intelligent women are a threat so let him feel he has the answers.

If it's not headed towards marriage you are wasting your time.

If he is jealous it means he loves you.

If he is possessive it means he loves you.

If he is abusive it means he loves you.

Buying a house together will save your relationship.

Get married. It will save your relationship.

Have a kid. It will save your relationship.

Give it time. He will change.

If you love him, change for him.

Watch him like a hawk.

Your significant other should be your highest, only priority.

He should be your everything.

Don't rock the boat.

Don't go to bed angry.

Love hurts.

Love means sacrifice.

Love is enough.

Love conquers all.

Boundaries for Introverts

"I need alone time."

"Thank you so much for inviting me! I won't be able to make it."

"I am not ready to talk about that."

"I will come over but will leave early."

"Let's set up some time to chat, but I can't talk for more than 30 minutes."

"I am feeling really burned out and need to keep to myself this weekend."

"I am sorry to cancel but I am feeling socially overwhelmed and need time to recover."

"I really want to see you but feel overextended. Can we do this next week instead?"

"Just because I need to be alone doesn't mean I don't want to be with you."

Why Is It Hard To Forgive?

Because —

Forgiving can feel like mourning.

Revenge can sound more satisfying.

Anger can feel more powerful.

Refusing to forgive can feel like control.

Forgiving can be confused for weakness.

Forgiving can feel like sentencing myself to being perpetually misunderstood.

Forgiving can feel like change I am not ready for.

Forgiving can feel like dredging all my feelings up again.

I consider forgiving = justifying.

I equate forgiving with cleaning the slate.

I relate forgiving with reconciling.

I consider forgiving opening myself up for a repeat of the same infraction.

I liken forgiving to having to let things go back to the way they once were.

IN THE END,
FORGIVENESS
IS A GIFT YOU
GIVE YOURSELF.

DEDA

When To Leave a Cheater

If the cheater is not sorry or remorseful.

If the cheater does not believe he (or she) did anything wrong.

If the cheater believes this is not really that big of a deal.

If the cheater has cheated repeatedly.

If the cheater is frequently lying.

If the cheater is defensive.

If the cheater blames the person they cheated on.

If the relationship has shown signs of being one-sided.

If you know you are in the presence of something you can never get past.

If you cannot communicate.

If one or both of you is not willing to do what it will take to heal.

If you don't consider your relationship worth the work it will take to repair.

If any of these things are true, forgive the cheater. Forgive, because forgiveness is for you. Forgive, then break up and don't look back. We all deserve someone worth trusting.

How To Show Empathy

Here is how:

A person says: *"Everything is unraveling."*

This is not empathy: *"Everything happens for a reason! "*

This is empathy: *"I understand why you feel this way."*

A person says: *"I don't see a way out."*

This is not empathy: *"Hey! Chin up!"*

This is empathy: *"I've seen you get out of really complicated situations before this one."*

A person says: *"We are all going to die."*

This is not empathy: *"Everything is going to be OK!"*

This is empathy: *"We are going through a scary time. It's OK to not be OK."*

A person says: *"I feel so sad."*

This is not empathy: *"OK, but no crying."*

This is empathy: *"All feelings are welcome here."*

A person says: "*We are doomed.*"

This is not empathy: "*I only allow optimism!*"

This is empathy: "*It does feel like doom. But a positive outcome is plausible.*"

A person says: "*I feel depressed.*"

This is not empathy: "*Let's go do something fun! FUN, FUN, FUN!*"

This is empathy: "*I am sorry. What can I do to support you?*"

A person says: "*Nothing good can come of this.*"

This is not empathy: "*You must learn to see the good.*"

This is empathy: "*It sure is hard to see right now. Let's take this one day at a time.*"

Trustworthy People

Solidity. Trustworthy people have a discipline, a transparency, a gravitas, an ease.

They tell themselves the truth. If they are honest with themselves they are more likely to be honest with others.

Trustworthy people listen, take in information, double-check. (For this reason, they are frequently right.)

A tendency to treat people with respect.

A practice of respecting the boundaries of others.

When they ask you for a favor they find a way to balance the scale. This is not a quid pro quo, but a natural tendency towards what is fair.

People who are thoughtful before being influenced by another. If I am easily influenced by others, my mind, my decisions and my actions will change according to the person I am with. Conversely, trustworthy people are able to change their minds as they learn new information.

Accountability. Listen to their stories. Do they take responsibility or is someone else always to blame?

They don't gossip or criticize. If I gossip to you about others, I gossip about you to others.

They know how to keep a secret. If I share with you someone else's secret, guess what I will do with yours?

They speak well of people around them, and people in their past. *"All my exes are crazy"* or *"all my friends were bad news"* is a flag.

Strong opinions, rather than a person picking what they say to match what you want to hear.

Taking sides. Beware of people who are all things to everyone.

Projection. I attribute to others actions and behaviors I tend to make myself, so what do I repeatedly attribute to others?

People you can trust are people who tend to connect, rather than isolate others. *"There is someone I'd like to introduce you to — you guys have similar interests."*

Trustworthy people in turn trust that as they give to the world, the world gives to them.

Boundaries With Family

"I am so excited for your visit! You can't stay in my house this time, but I can recommend a few hotels nearby."

"When you come visit, make sure you make plans of your own because I won't be able to spend full days with you."

"If you want my brother to do something, can you suggest it to him directly?"

"We believe in different things. Please do not impose your beliefs on me."

"Please stop asking when I will get married — have a child — have another child. You have made clear these things are important to you, but they are private to me and my significant other."

"I do not want to discuss that subject but we can talk about other things."

"Please don't serve me enormous amounts of food. I will serve myself, thank you."

"Please don't look through my things. If you want to borrow something, please ask me."

"Please don't raise your voice at me or use threatening or diminishing language or I will have to leave."

263

Fear of Abandonment

I find it hard to trust. First, myself, then other people.

I am always feeling like my significant other has lost interest and doesn't love me anymore, like he has discovered I'm not as great as he once thought I was. I guess the gig is up.

I am intolerant of any form of criticism — if I feel like the other person perceives me as imperfect, why would they want to stay?

I crave a lot of reassurance. No amount of "I love you" feels like enough.

I feel unlovable or unworthy. How could anyone love me, if I am awful?

I get attached fast and deep and tend to give too much.

I often find myself in one-sided relationships.

I feel suspicious, possessive and jealous because I believe someone else can easily take what I have.

I compare myself to others and feel I always fall short.

I feel scared, angry, and resentful if my significant other does things that do not involve me.

A small fight feels to me like the end of a relationship; like the loss will be nothing less than total.

If someone is moody, unhappy, restless, I conclude it must be something I did.

I overthink.

I fear and therefore avoid separation. Even *"I am leaving now but will see you tomorrow"* makes me feel angsty.

I struggle with transitions.

I people please and set no boundaries. Because, I want you to like me.

I remain in relationships that are not good for me because I think it's impossible that anyone else will want me.

I jump quickly from one relationship to another, often beginning one before the other ends.

I Am Unsafe If —

I see the world through my insecurities so believe the problem is you instead of me. I might say *"nobody understands me"* or *"why does this always happen to me?"*

I blame everyone but me. Taking responsibility is one of the biggest characteristics of a person who is safe.

I put others down because it makes me feel better about myself. This includes judgment, criticism, gossip, the compulsion to give unwanted advice while telling myself I am "trying to help".

I have to have the final word: I need to always be right and need to know more than you.

I cannot apologize, or say "I'm sorry" but only as a formality (*"I am sorry you feel that way!"*). People who mean it when they say they are sorry accompany the apology with a noticeable effort to change their behavior.

I need to fix everything and try to bend reality to make me comfortable rather than making space for how you are actually feeling. (You: *"I am anxious."* Me: *"No! Don't be anxious! Look at the bright side! It all happens for a reason!"*)

I lie. I tell myself that most of my lies are "white lies" intended to protect others. It is unsafe to live in a world another person is fabricating for us. We all deserve to live in a world that is real.

Handling Difficult Conversations

The first, most helpful lesson I've learned about handling difficult conversations is the knowledge that two people can hold contradictory opinions and both be right. Another person can have a different experience, a different perspective, and I can hold both that one and mine without feeling like mine is being threatened.

The second best lesson I have learned about how to handle a difficult conversation is that I can take a break. If I feel emotionally depleted and like I can't think anymore, I can say *"can we please continue this at another time?"*

I begin the conversation with a very clear sense of what I want: I don't want to be right. I don't want to win. I want to be heard, and understood. This charges the conversation differently than if I am approaching it like it's war.

We take turns. Your point of view, then my point of view. No monologues. No one sided arguments. No talking over one another.

I make an effort to listen. This means really listen — not pretend to listen while thinking about something else, or thinking about how I'm right, or thinking about how I will defend myself.

Speaking of which, I try to not be defensive. This is extremely hard — it means setting aside my primal instinct in an effort to make understanding the other person a priority.

I use sentences that start with "I" and refer to my feelings, rather than statements that start with "you" and are critical of the other person. *"I feel alone when you don't back me up"* will get a very different reaction than *"you are a traitor!"*

I focus on one thing at a time. I try to refrain from bringing up that time when you___, or the seven other times when you have___, or you always____, or you never___.

Respect is a big part of the deal. No swearing. No putting the other down. No raising of voices. No throwing things. Of course, no violence.

And, I tell the truth. Lying means pretending the difficult conversation is about something else. When someone has been lying to me, I look back and see how we never really talked about what we needed to.

269

Emotional Boundaries

I am feeling overwhelmed so I'm going to give myself some time alone. Can we catch up next week?

I am taking a break from social media.

I am creating a social media feed that does not bring me down so am unfollowing accounts that give an unrealistic impression about what real life is like.

I am only reading the news a couple of times a week to better manage the onslaught of negativity that I expose myself to.

I do not watch crime shows, horror movies or thrillers.

I don't need advice but I need to talk through something. I wonder if you can just listen without trying to fix things for me?

I am dealing with the illness of someone I love and am overwhelmed by people who ask how he is doing when he will never get better. Can you say *"I am here for you"* instead of *"how is he?"*

Thank you for your support but I am not ready to talk about my breakup.

That is a personal question and I am not going to answer it.

I cannot instantly reply to your texts.

I love you very much but if you snap at me when you are angry I am going to have to call a time out.

I need to take things slow.

I need to clarify where this relationship is going.

Can we talk about that tomorrow? This conversation has the potential to upset me and I don't want it to disrupt my sleep.

I turn off my phone in the late afternoon so I can have quiet evenings.

My answer is no, and I don't have to explain myself.

The Opposite of Codependency

The ability to recognize my worth regardless of what others think or how they feel about me.

The practice of advocating for myself, which requires an intimate understanding of what I need and want so I know what to advocate for.

Self-compassion: treating myself like I would treat the person I love and care for the most.

Boundaries. Understanding them, setting them, enforcing them, respecting the boundaries of others.

The ability to separate saying "no" and how important you are to me. The ability to hear your "no" and not associate it with my worth or your feelings for me.

The desire for time alone.

The opposite of codependency is the practice of learning how to love myself and how to conceive of myself as separate and sovereign from you.

YOU

ME

DZDR

What To Do if I'm Hurt by Someone I Love

When someone I love hurts my feelings the first thing I (try to) do is pause.

Giving myself a time out grants me the space to really look at what happened. Did this person intend to hurt me? Was this just clumsy? Does it happen a lot? Was it something hard that I needed to hear?

Looking inside myself allows me to put things in their just place and approach this in a way that is more thoughtful and less reactive.

This might sound like *"I need to take some time to myself to process what you said. I am hurt right now and time will allow me to approach this matter in a more constructive way."*

Then, I attempt to remove all aggression from my reaction. I try to not be righteous, accusatory, hostile, or defensive. I stand a better chance of understanding if I listen, and a better chance at being understood if I can explain my perspective calmly.

Even if it's really hard I push myself to talk about what happened. Rather than saying nothing, I might start with *"What you did/said really hurt my feelings."* It's important I show me I will stand up for myself.

Then, *"I wonder if you can explain why you said what you said. I want to understand it better but I also want to understand your motivation for saying it."*

Hopefully this makes room for a conversation that is open, receptive, constructive, clear and healing. Hopefully it brings us closer together.

Finally, boundaries. If there is a pattern of hurtful behavior or a reluctance to see it, recognize it, acknowledge it or work on it, I might resort to saying something like *"what you said/did was really hurtful. Please stop hurting me or I will need to distance myself from this relationship."*

What To Say if Someone Asks if You Love Them and You Don't

Some options (to say only if they are true):

I do not.

I don't feel the same way.

I don't love you and do not foresee this changing in the future.

I don't feel the same way now, but I feel like I'm just getting to know you.

I don't love you, but I like you a lot.

I don't love you but you matter to me a lot.

I don't love you in the romantic sense, but I love you very much as a friend.

DEDR

What Causes Conflict?

My inevitable lack of self-awareness.

I am angry to begin with and take it out on you because I am powerless to take it out on who I'm really angry with.

You press my buttons and/or I press yours so I am angry at you but mostly you have activated something that happened a long time ago which throws everything out of proportion.

I am projecting.

I am not being clear, to you or to myself.

I am not being honest, to you or to myself.

I am not listening. I think I don't know how.

I am not taking responsibility.

I want to fix you.

I put you down.

I blame you. This is on you.

I am not expressing my limit so you cross it.

I am expressing my limit and you cross it anyway.

You are expressing your limit and I am not respecting it.

You are not expressing your limit and I unknowingly push on it.

I don't feel safe.

I am defensive.

We have no time away from each other. Time away
is perspective.

Instead of allowing for your point of view, I want to hurt you.

Instead of listening, I want you to think like I think.

Instead of understanding, I want to win.

Instead of getting to know you, I want you to be who I think
you are.

How To Stop People From Trying To Set You Up

"Please don't attempt to set me up with anyone. I don't like it."

"I know you mean well, but please stop trying to set me up with someone. It's not what I want and I find it invasive."

"I know that when you try to set me up with someone you are trying to 'help' but it makes me feel like you believe my lifestyle needs correcting."

"When you try to set me up with someone you are going against what I have chosen for myself."

"I have told you in the past not to try to set me up. If you continue to do so I am going to have to stop seeing you for a while."

"I have told you many times not to set me up with others. If this comes up again I will have to leave."

Why Do Couples Break Up After a Long Time?

I don't love you.

I don't like you.

I don't trust you.

I don't know you.

I don't know me.

We are not friends anymore.

We are not connected.

Everything changes and we have not changed in the same direction.

We don't share ourselves.

We are different and our differences are irreconcilable.

I have finally realized I cannot change you so this is me giving up.

We are not compatible.

We both prioritize you.

I love you and breaking up with you is me standing up for myself as I feel I deserve the things you don't give me.

Indifference.

Signs Someone Will Not Treat You Well

I notice how this person talks to themselves, in particular if they are aware of the difference between their own voice and that of their ego.

I notice how this person talks about others, in particular as it relates to accountability and assigning blame.

I notice how this person treats other people, those close to him and those that are in a position that holds less power.

I notice how this person reacts when I set a boundary that works for me but that perhaps is not convenient to them.

I notice how this person treats animals.

How Do We Disrespect Ourselves?

Speaking to myself in a way I would never speak to a friend.

Not expressing what I want or need.

Saying yes to everything, and ending up overextended, overwhelmed and resentful.

Any expression of an absence of boundaries.

Overexplaining.

Accepting aggression or hurtful behavior due to fear of change (or for any reason).

Nearly any action driven by fear.

Complaining, instead of working on improving what I'm complaining about.

Pretending I like something I don't like.

Any attempt to fit in.

Forcing anything.

Trying to fix someone other than me.

Not caring for myself, in particular if I know I really need that care. (If I am particularly anxious, for example.)

Being hyper-invested in anyone who clearly doesn't feel the same about me.

SIGNS YOU'RE DISRESPECTING YOURSELF.

SPEAKING BADLY TO YOURSELF.

YOU'RE SUCH AN AWFUL PERSON!

NOT EXPRESSING WHAT YOU NEED.

NO.

I'M NOT THIRSTY.

SAYING YES TO EVERYTHING.

YES YES YES
YES YES
YES YES
YES YES

ABSENCE OF BOUNDARIES.

LOOK, NO BOUNDARIES!

OVER-EXPLAINING.

WELL, SEE WHAT I MEANT HAS TO SAY THAT NO IDEA IT WAS GOING TO...

ACTING FROM FEAR.

BOO!

COMPLAINING.

IT ALL SUCKS!

PRETENDING TO LIKE IT.

THANK YOU.

ATTEMPTING TO FIT IN.

TRYING TO FIX SOMEONE ELSE.

I CAN FIX YOU!

NOT CARING FOR YOURSELF.

OVER-INVESTED EMOTIONALLY.

BUT I LOVE YOU SO MUCH!

D2DR

Why Is Receiving Hard?

It can feel —

Like I am ceasing to protect something that needs to be defended.

Like a loss of control.

Like now I am vulnerable.

Like I am leaving myself open to being manipulated.

Like there's got to be a catch.

Like now I owe you something.

Like now you have a right to want something from me.

Like I am selfish.

Like I am getting attention I don't want.

Like shame.

Like I now feel self-conscious.

Like I have done nothing to deserve this.

Like now I am overwhelmed.

Like this is too much.

285

What Is 'Crossing Boundaries'?

If someone tries to kiss me and I say no and they kiss me anyway they have crossed my boundary.

If I say *"I am not going to see you today because I have a lot of work"* and they show up at my house they are crossing a boundary.

If I say *"I cannot work on Sunday"* and someone puts a meeting on the calendar for Sunday they are crossing a boundary.

If I say *"I don't want to talk about my relationship"* and someone asks me questions about my relationship they are crossing a boundary.

If I say *"I am not really looking for advice"* and someone keeps telling me what I should do they are crossing a boundary.

If I say *"I am not really in a place where I can listen"* and someone talks nonstop for 30 minutes, they are crossing a boundary.

If I say *"I am feeling overwhelmed so am going to stay home"* and they say *"Come on! Live a little!"* they are crossing a boundary.

If I say *"I will spend the first 15 minutes of each day breathing and stretching"* and instead I wake up and grab my phone I am crossing my own boundary.

286

How To Let Go of Ego

To "let go" of ego, first you have to recognize her. (Or him, as the case may be.)

Have you ever wondered who "wears the pants" in your relationship? Ego.

Do you control, maneuver, manipulate? Ego.

Do you feel indignant, huffy? Ego.

Do you want to be right, have the upper hand? Ego.

Do you think about how to get back at something he did? Ego.

Do you want you two to agree on everything, to have identical opinions? Ego.

When you fight, do you fight to be understood, heard, to defend yourself? Ego.

Do you expect him to guess what you need? I mean, he should just know, right? Ego.

Do you want to fix, save, rescue, help, improve, advise? Ego.

Do you want him to change? Ego.

Are you hungry for attention, for others to find you attractive? Ego.

Do you want to find in others what he does not give you? Ego.

Do you feel like he belongs to you? Do you feel jealous, possessive, territorial? Ego.

Do you expect him to alter his behavior to accommodate your emotions? Ego.

Do you have strong opinions of what he should or shouldn't do? Ego.

Do you want to win? Ego.

Becoming aware of ego is the only real catalyst for change.

Psychological Abuse

If someone wants to hurt you, scare you, control you, confuse you or diminish your self-esteem, this is defined as psychological abuse.

A few obvious examples are threats to harm you, humiliate you, manipulate you or leave you.

But sometimes psychological abuse is harder to detect, in particular if someone alternates abuse with seeming caring.

Here are a few examples of what it might look like:

"Wow, you are so dramatic. Just take a breath," or *"I was just kidding! Learn how to take a joke!"* This shows a tendency to ignore, minimize or refuse to accept how something makes you feel.

"You are my chubby little hippo!" or any pet name that puts you down.

"I know you are trying but maybe this is not something you can grasp," or any commentary that is patronizing, derogatory.

"Aren't you too old to be doing that?" Anything that puts down what you are interested in or that brings you joy.

"Did you have fun at the park at lunchtime today?" Anything that makes you feel you are being monitored is a form of abuse.

"Everybody thinks you haven't been yourself lately." People who abuse you frequently use others to do so to throw you off.

"I don't want you to dress like that/I don't want you to see your friends/you are too close to your family." All these examples can be attempts to control you.

"I don't think you should hang out with your friends anymore — I want more time for us." Trying to isolate you or separate you from people who love you.

"What you are describing did not take place." This is denying someone else's experience, which can leave you second-guessing yourself.

"Well, if you don't want me to throw things, then don't do things you know will upset me!" This shifts the responsibility of their behavior onto you, making you wonder if it's all your fault.

"You are not qualified for that." Be careful of anyone who does not support you or makes less of anything you want to accomplish. Healthy relationships build rather than sabotage your self-esteem.

"If you leave me I will kill myself." This is coercion, a form of intimidation, and designed to scare you.

Find your feet. Trust yourself. Set boundaries. Say no.

Abuse is never your fault.

Distance yourself from anyone who makes you feel you deserve to be treated poorly, who makes you wonder about your self-worth, or your sanity.

How To Ask Someone to Mind Their Own Business

"I do not want to talk about X at all but I am happy to instead talk about Y."

"Before I even begin I want to clarify that I want you to listen and do not want you to fix things."

"I am not looking for advice. I am working on figuring this out on my own."

"I know you are coming from a good place. But, understandably I am not open to another person's opinion on something so integral to my own life."

"What you are suggesting is not right for me."

"If I need advice I promise I will straight up ask for it. Right now advice is not what I need."

"I am grateful you are worried about me but you worrying is making me feel burdened rather than cared for."

"I need you to trust that I can take care of myself."

"I can see you are trying to help. This thing you are doing is not helpful. What would instead be helpful is ___."

"I can see you want to be useful. What I could really use right now is ___."

291

"I am definitely not going to do that."

"We disagree."

"No."

What Does It Mean To Be Grown Up?

You know how to manage your own emotions and trust yourself.

You make you happy.

You are aware of your own triggers, insecurities, expectations, assumptions and projections.

You regard yourself and the other as flawed.

You know how to communicate and don't expect the other to have extrasensory perception.

You express rather than hide or diminish what you feel.

You don't avoid "difficult" or "awkward." That's how you grow.

You understand two people can have different opinions, even conflicting ones, and both be right.

You know it's ok to disagree.

You are quick to say *"I was wrong, and I am sorry."*

You know how to say no without fear.

You both identify and ask for what you need.

You don't blame or accuse.

You don't fight to win or maim. You fight to understand.

You wield the power of pausing.

You give each other space, time apart, privacy, sovereignty.

You rejoice when the other does well.

You acknowledge that "grown up" is fleeting at best and both recognize and forgive yourself when you act like a four year old. Or maybe this is just me.

What Happens When We Stop Pleasing?

My entire relationship landscape is directly related to my behavior.

If I am a people-pleaser and work to change this, naturally my relationship landscape will change as a result.

The first people who will disappear will be those who grew comfortable benefiting from me sacrificing my needs to meet theirs.

I feel alone and wonder if this is worthwhile if all I want is to be loved and accepted by the people who are important to me.

At first this is painful but I stand up for myself and trust that I have begun a process that is good for me and ultimately good for my relationships too.

Yep. This is worthwhile.

I begin to behave like me. I am not pretending to be someone I am not, acting like I like things I don't like, claiming to be interested in things that don't interest me at all. If I don't want to do something, I say no.

I can say no!

The quality of my relationships begins to improve. We move beyond small talk, beyond gossip, beyond judgment, into experiences that run deeper and are more connected to who I am.

The people I surround myself with have a similar rhythm to me. They too want and need time to themselves, are involved in things besides me.

Dynamics feel relaxed, easy, rather than charged with an intensity that tends to flame out.

I find it easier to place boundaries and become aware of how I react to the boundaries of others.

I spend time with my friends and feel supremely accepted, re-energized rather than overextended, resentful and exhausted.

What Does It Mean To Take It Slow?

When someone says "let's take it slow" here are some of the things it can mean:

I feel you are ready for more than I am ready for.

I don't know if I am interested.

I want to get to know you better.

I am not sure.

I am not ready to commit to you.

I am afraid.

I am uncomfortable.

I want to protect myself from this.

I am not ready to have sex.

We had sex, but I don't feel a connection.

I really like you, and I don't want to mess this up.

I don't have room for you in my life.

I don't have room for you in my life and need to get it together.

If someone says "let's take it slow" and you don't know what it means, the only way to find out is to talk about it.

Some questions to ask: *"What do you mean? What does the right pace look like to you?"*

Now, what if you are the one feeling things might be moving a bit too fast? Here are a few questions to ask yourself:

Are you portraying yourself as you really are?

Are you telling the truth?

Are you setting boundaries?

Are you suddenly neglecting any part of your life?

If any of these things are happening, take some time to yourself. Communicate as clearly as you can. Be as honest as you can.

And remember that the only ones who can set the relationship on a rhythm that is just right are the two people inside the relationship.

DZDR

Can Loving a Person Too Much Push Them Away?

If I intensely love you and my feelings for myself depend on how you feel about me,

if I expect you to be everything, play every role, meet every need,

if I hold you responsible for my state of mind,

if I want to either save you or be saved by you,

if I must control you,

if leaving to do other things makes me feel anxious or abandoned,

if I cannot spend time alone,

I will push you away.

If I intensely love you and also love myself independently of how you feel about me,

if I love you but meet my own needs,

if we communicate clearly,

if we enjoy spending time without each other,

if being alone feels peaceful and necessary,

then our love can be as big as this galaxy and contiguous ones
and I will not push you away.

The way we love either nourishes or suffocates.

It's never love — in any amount — that pushes others away.

We Are Not One

Nothing is more important than my relationship with me. Working on myself is the only lasting way to improve my relationships with others. (Insecurity corrupts my ability to accept healthy love.)

An enormous green flag is a partner who is working on himself. He has follow through, is dependable, speaks well of others, knows what he wants and can clearly express it.

The result of us working on ourselves is a healthy system we create together.

I do not define myself through what he or others think of me, and neither does he.

I know that boundaries (clear lines of separation to protect our own limits) make us stronger. Saying yes to everything to get the other person to stay has never been effective.

My emotions are mine and my responsibility. His emotions are his and his responsibility. My happiness is not on him. His jealousy is not on me (and is not a sign that he loves me).

We can and do have different opinions and don't feel the need to agree on everything.

To get what I want or need I communicate clearly because the other person cannot "just know". Learning to communicate clearly is the only way for others to understand what I think, feel and want.

Who I want another person to be is not who they are. Who I want them to be is not their responsibility. We do not attempt to change, fix, improve or save each other.

I do not control other people. Others cannot try to control me.

We both need time alone, as the separate, sovereign beings that we are.

Is It Love or Ego?

Ego:

I want to be right.

I want to be better than you.

I want you to be better and I want you to do it for me.

I want you to behave the way I want you to.

I want you to make me happy.

I want you to understand me.

I want you to see me.

I want to fix you.

Boundaries are so selfish.

I play games to make you feel jealous or like you might lose me.

I am angry when you take me for granted.

Drama is romantic.

Love:

I accept I am flawed.

I love you just the way you are.

I expect you to be flawed because you are human.

Boundaries = healthy relationship.

I am responsible for my evolution and my happiness and support your evolution and your happiness.

I communicate as clearly as I can.

I want what's best for you.

Why Do People Break Their Vows?

Boredom. Ennui. A deep-seated, long standing indifference. Carelessness. Callousness. Distraction. I am not thinking about my vows. I am thinking about this.

An overbearing sense that every day is the same, that life has no meaning and that there has to be more to it than this.

Anhedonia. Numbness. Emptiness. Despair.

Hunger — a ravenous hunger for experiences.

A sense of entitlement. I deserve this.

Insatiability. I think I have everything but I want more.

Fear.

Power.

What Do Non-Codependent People Do?

A non-codependent person:

Enjoys the pleasure of her own company.

Has strong, clear, elastic boundaries and is comfortable saying no.

Is guided by what she thinks she should do, rather than what would make others happy or more comfortable.

Has both confidence and self-awareness.

Communicates clearly without fear of being judged, put down or criticized.

Is able to keep herself separate from others: your emotions are not my emotions, it is safe for us to disagree or perceive things differently, you can hurt me and hurting me does not necessarily mean you did something wrong.

Easily makes decisions.

Takes care of herself.

Trusts herself.

Finds that drama and chaos are not interesting.

Recognizes that spending time gossiping or putting others down might feel like connection when in fact it is not.

Understands that how others express themselves and how others behave defines them, not her.

Spends no time managing what others think of her.

Understands disappointing others and being misunderstood are inevitable.

Willingly holds difficult conversations.

Is adroit at managing conflict.

Experiences no anxiety in separation.

Knows that better relationships start with a better relationship with herself.

I GOT YOU.

Wrong Reasons To Stay in a Relationship

Because I am afraid.

Because I don't like change.

Because I don't want anyone to get hurt.

Because leaving is the same as failing.

Because I feel guilty.

Because it's complicated.

Because I feel comfortable.

Because I am miserable but it's misery I know.

Because this is the life I am destined to live.

Because I have already invested so much.

Because this is as good as it will get.

Because I will never find anyone else.

Because it's bad but any minute now it will get better.

Because starting over takes too much effort.

Because anything is better than being alone.

311

What's an Avoidant-Dismissive Partner Like?

Dismissive avoidant people are very independent. The person they want to rely on the most is themselves.

Getting too close feels to them like being thrown into a prison. You are constantly being pushed away.

Feeling dependent feels dangerous to them.

Feeling controlled feels intolerable.

They constantly feel their freedom is being threatened. *"Stop pressuring me!"*

Intimacy, vulnerability and emotions feel unsafe.

They find it difficult to articulate their feelings.

Withdrawing is easier than expressing their needs.

They are terrified of commitment. As such, romantic entanglements tend to not be their priority.

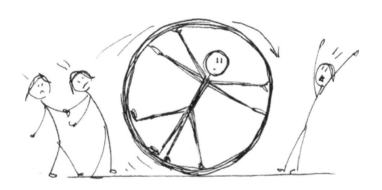

313

Why Do We Push Others' Boundaries?

I push on another's boundaries because I don't know what they are.

Because pushing on another's boundaries is human nature.

Because I want you to do what I want you to do, not what you want to do.

This is how I know that once I draw a boundary with someone I know I have to draw it over and over. Because, just as I push on another's boundary, others will do it to me.

Of course, there is a difference between a boundary pusher and a boundary intimidator, a smasher, someone who shows no respect to what I said my limits were.

Depending on how acute the situation is, this might make me decide to keep my distance, so I can safeguard my peace of mind. It doesn't matter who they are.

What Is the Point of a Relationship if You Have Nothing in Common?

Adventure. Life is wider and richer than the limits of my own preferences.

To become a better person.

To create love.

To learn about myself.

To learn about the mystery that is the person I love.

To live within the privileged confines of a healthy challenge.

To learn I can wholeheartedly support someone even if we see things differently.

Company.

Camaraderie.

Sharing.

Intimacy.

Sex.

To foster a partner in accountability.

To develop my communication skills.

To exercise my ability to determine what I want.

To reinforce every day my boundary-setting skills.

To widen my perspective.

To learn every day how to see things differently.

To be reminded every day how two people can do and like and believe different things and both be right.

To rejoice in the ability to disagree and still feel safe.

To learn new things.

To grow.

To have fun.

To feel understood despite the lack of common ground.

To better grasp where I am willing to sacrifice, where I am willing to compromise and where I am not.

To learn how to think about what someone else wants, not only what I want.

To get to taste things in a restaurant that I would never order.

How Can I Know if a Friend Is Worth Keeping?

I would keep a close eye on:

One-sided relationships.

Friends who place unreasonable expectations on you, so that it feels like you are falling short rather than in the company of someone you love.

Friends who put you down, tease you in a way that is demeaning, expose, embarrass you or constantly question your worth.

Friends who see you as someone to hang out with, rather than as someone unique and valuable.

Friends who are possessive and separate you from other friends.

Friends who instead of supporting your efforts find a way to sabotage them, like insisting you have a drink when you said you were not drinking.

Friends who disrespect your boundaries.

Friends who leave you feeling exhausted.

Friends who are not happy for you when something wonderful happens to you.

To me, it's less about severing relationships and more about making more room for more loving, supportive friends.

What Makes Certain Conversations "Harder" Than Others?

I feel confused about how I feel.

I don't know how to say what I want to say.

I feel strong feelings: angry, hurt, misunderstood, unheard.

I don't want to fight.

I don't want to lose something important.

I don't like confrontation.

I don't want to hurt your feelings.

I don't want my feelings to get hurt.

I don't want to be misunderstood.

I don't want to feel shame.

I don't want you to think less of me.

I don't want to lose.

I don't want to lose you.

I don't want things to change between us.

I don't want to say the wrong thing.

I don't want you to think it's my fault.

I want to be understood and I worry that you won't.

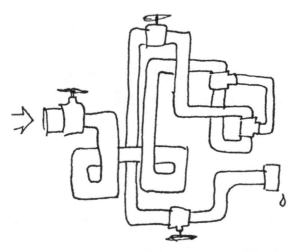

IT'S EASY TO MAKE THINGS HARD.

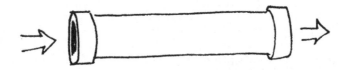

IT'S HARD TO MAKE THINGS EASY.

Can You Tell Me How To Love?

I step into the fact that I am 50% the creator, architect and designer of every one of my relationships. We are a system and as such it's not the other person who is toxic or ___.

If I am disconnected from myself I am more likely to place unrealistic expectations on my relationships. (Complete me! Make me happy! Fix me! Love me unconditionally!)

I remind myself every day I cannot change other people. I can't change their mind, I can't change who they are, I can't change what they want, and I can't change how they live. I cannot change how they love me.

I can and do work on being a better person. Working on me is the only way to work on my relationships so it's sound logic to look for relationships with people interested in working on themselves. I don't want you to make me happy. I want you to give me the space I need to become a better me.

I do not expect any milestone to change what I have right now. Marriage will not increase our level of commitment. Babies will not fix us.

I establish boundaries. Without them, I invite resentment into my relationship dynamics, feel taken advantage of, wonder why my generosity is repaid so poorly.

I am as honest, as transparent and clear as I can possibly be.

I do not expect perfection — from me or from anyone else. Whenever I do (because, I'm not perfect) I recognize my expectation is lying to me.

The best thing I can do for any relationship with anyone is to learn how to love myself.

How Do You Sincerely Apologize?

If I am apologizing, here are the things I try to keep out of the apology:

Any excuse or justification.

Any lying.

Any ignoring or minimizing any part of what happened.

Examples of statements that are not apologies:

"But I already said I was sorry."

"I am sorry you feel that way."

"I am sorry you interpreted things in the way you did."

"I am sorry for what happened."

"I did not mean to upset you."

"This was not really my fault."

Elements that convey sincerity in the apology: acceptance and full responsibility.

Listen without being defensive.

Fully admit you were wrong.

Add that you understand that what you did was hurtful.

Say you are sorry and explore if there are any ways to undo or atone for what you did.

Don't do it again — a true apology goes hand in hand with a change in behavior. Without this change, "I'm sorry" is just a form of manipulation.

Leave the door open — *"If there is anything else you want to tell me, I am all ears."*

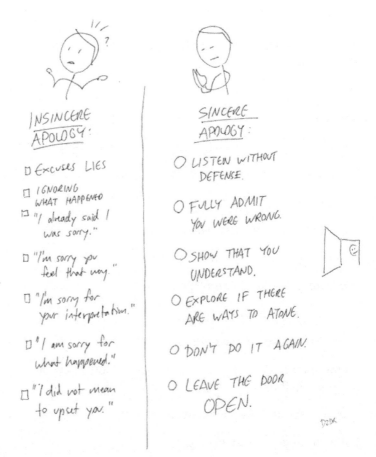

324

What Does Nobody Tell You About Relationships?

You won't always be happy.

"Happily ever after" does not just happen.

"Perfect" does not exist. Flaws in the other person are inevitable.

Flaws in you are inevitable. Also, there is nothing wrong with you.

Disappointment is inevitable.

Being misunderstood is inevitable.

Relationships are more about growth than they are about happiness.

Relationships are constantly changing, like the ocean.

It's not about fighting less but about learning how to manage conflict.

"Let's take a break" is healthier than *"let's not go to bed angry."*

Listening is not about fixing.

Clearly expressing your needs is more important than compromise. (Compromise is not about giving in, which breeds resentment. It's about ensuring everyone feels seen, heard, understood, and respected. This cannot take place if I am not clearly expressing my needs.)

Defending ourselves from perceived attacks makes it difficult to communicate respectfully.

Self-awareness is key to avoid being hurtful.

Kindness is relationship super-glue.

We tend to notice the negative. For a relationship to survive, we need to notice the positive. What do you talk more about: things the other keeps doing wrong, or things you want to say thank you for?

"My god. You are wonderful. Thank you for loving me."

Recovering People-Pleaser

I am a recovering people-pleaser and the reason I became one in the first place is because I believed it was the only way to survive.

I need others, and if I could make them find me useful, helpful, valuable, then I could prevent them from leaving.

Sacrificing my own needs and fixing others was the only way I knew how to create relationships.

Feeling like I wasn't needed made me question if there was even a point to my existence.

Any attempt to stop being a people-pleaser was not only terrifying: it was painful.

Feeling misunderstood felt like the worst kind of isolation: like being abandoned on an old, crumbling ship in the middle of a turbulent ocean.

Feeling criticized felt like I could never get anything right.

Not getting the fix of validation I needed made me question everything.

Mustering up the courage to say no — or attempting to set any boundary — made me feel like a horrible, selfish person, made me feel guilty and disloyal.

The name of this extremely common behavior is "codependency". The "cure" to all of this is learn how to love myself, to set boundaries, to recognize that saying no is the only way to create healthy relationships, even if it feels counterintuitive.

The more I practice, the easier it becomes.

How Do I Know if I Am a Rebound?

Does the person you are dating seem in touch with themselves? Can you clearly identify who they are, what matters to them, their tastes, preferences, wants, interests, aspirations?

How long ago did the person you are dating end their previous relationship?

Do things feel solid, consistent? Does the person you are dating follow through on what they say they are going to do?

Set aside any emotions or feelings related to sheer attraction or chemistry. Set aside sex. How much is left?

How quickly are things moving? For example, is the person you are dating claiming they love you before they even know you?

Does the relationship feel healthy and fun or exhausting, like an emotional roller coaster?

Toxic Relationship Habits

I hold grudges and keep bringing up infractions in every argument. I use words like "always" and "never".

I am unaware of my own insecurities, so demand others alter their behavior to accommodate my fear and jealousy. I put people down to feel better about myself.

If someone tells me how something I did made them feel, defending myself takes precedence over listening.

I lie. Lies, white lies and lies by omission are how I handle any problem.

If I ever say "I'm sorry" I am vague about what I am apologizing for and do not change my behavior.

I blame instead of taking responsibility.

Lists of Questions To Get To Know Yourself Better
(Ideal for a Journal!)

Everyday Hero

How many times does the person that you love have a completely different opinion than yours and instead of saying *"no"* you say *"I am open"*?

How many times do you set aside whatever pressing thing you have to say just so you can listen?

How many times do you listen to understand the other rather than to design what you are going to say next?

How many times have you made understanding another take precedence over defending yourself?

How many times are you lucid enough to recognize the difference between *"you hurt me"* and *"you did something wrong"*?

How many times do you set aside fear and assume the best of the other?

How many times do you stop to realize you look for things to complain about more than you look for things to be appreciative about in the behavior of others?

How many times are you hurting and make an effort to recognize what you are really feeling?

How many times do you communicate clearly enough to say *"I want to put this into words but I don't know how"*?

How many times do you step into having a difficult conversation?

How many times have you said *"I was wrong, and I am sorry"*; defied the belief that these words somehow diminish you?

How many times do you admit that you need help?

How many times have you said *"This is really scary, but I'm going to keep coming back, because that's what commitment means"*?

HAPPY HALLOWEEN, HEROES! — DZDR

I am dazzled by flashy acts of heroism, but it's the every day in relationships that's relentless. It requires so much courage, and so much work.

That's the center of operations of the everyday hero.

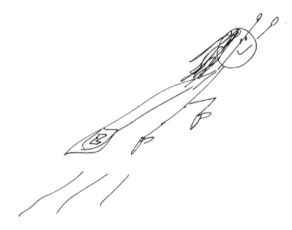

Good Friend or Bad?

Do you like them, and do you feel like they like you? I know this question sounds obvious, but what happens when you examine it?

Does your friendship seem stuck in another time — like the things you had in common are no longer present — or does it evolve as you evolve?

Do you like who you are when you are with them?

Do you feel accepted for who you are?

Do you feel criticized or supported?

Is their presence consistent or conditional? Does the relationship feel one-sided or balanced?

Do you trust them? Do they do what they say they are going to do? Do they ever use things you've said in confidence against you?

Are they quick to recognize when they've done something that has hurt you?

Are you good at communicating? Talking, sharing, but also expressing difficult things, saying you are sorry?

Do you feel the presence of envy or a tendency to compete?

Does your relationship have clear boundaries? Are they both firm and elastic? Are they respected?

Does your success make them happy?

Would your friend answer these questions the same way you would?

Alcoholic

Do I drink to cope? To feel better, to feel numb, to not feel pain, to not worry, to not feel anxious, to forget?

If I need alcohol every time I feel something every human frequently feels, I am at risk. I will feel this way again, and will drink again, only to feel this way again.

When I drink, do I black out? Do I forget the events that took place? Do I forget what I did?

How often do I think about the next drink?

Am I having trouble controlling how much I am drinking?

Do I lie to others or to myself about how much I am drinking?

Is my drinking having an impact on my life? Am I failing to show up for important things or for important people?

Once I see alcohol is impacting my life, is my response to drink again?

Is alcohol contributing to me making poor choices, such as drinking and driving?

Do I need to drink more to get the buzz I used to get from just one drink?

Does not drinking feel awful? Am I irritable? Am I either buzzed or hung over?

Do I want to drink more than wanting to do anything else?

The most obvious stage is when drinking completely takes over my life — I give it everything. My relationships, my health, my money, my time. But, alcoholism starts much earlier than this. I can do something about it much earlier than this.

Self-Value

Self-value is not stationary. I have good days and I have bad days.

In an effort to have more good days, here are the ways I check in with myself:

Am I giving my thoughts and my feelings a place or am I putting myself down for thinking and feeling them?

Am I identifying what I need or am I sacrificing what I need? Am I a good advocate for me?

Am I making healthy choices?

How quick am I to own up to a mistake and apologize for it?

Am I in relationships that feel one-sided, where I don't feel appreciated, where I am constantly exerting effort to be liked or loved?

Do I feel like setting boundaries is too risky, like if I say no I might lose the people who are important to me?

Does the behavior of others define me? (For example, believing that if you don't love me anymore that makes me unlovable.)

Do the opinions of others define me? (For example, believing that your appraisal of me is fact, rather than just your opinion.)

Am I refusing to accept a compliment but allowing criticism to hurt me or make me doubt myself?

Am I proud of myself and my efforts regardless of the results?

Do I compare myself to others?

Am I emotionally available?

How often do I make an effort to learn something new?

Do I feel like I need to settle for less because I'm not going to get it anyway?

Do I at any level believe I don't deserve good things?

Am I making myself small, hiding my personality, silencing myself?

There is no universal answer to the meaning of life. Have I given any thought to what the meaning of mine is?

Can I Trust Myself?

Do you believe you are worth loving?

If someone believes something about you, do you believe it to be true, or do you make room for the fact that what people say is more a reflection of themselves?

If you hear a belief contrary to your own are you open to changing your mind or do you feel threatened?

Do you question your own beliefs?

When making decisions, do you pause and reflect, maybe sleep on things, or do you seek advice and opinions?

How do you feel when your own opinions are not considered? Like you don't matter, or like maybe you deserve to surround yourself with people who consider what you have to say to be of value?

Do you spend a lot of time trying to control other people?

Do you spend a lot of time trying to control how people perceive you?

Do you follow through on what you say you are going to do, finish what you start?

The answer to these questions should help you find the answer you are looking for.

Signs of a Person's Character

Listen. How does this person talk about others? How much judgment can you hear? Blame? Criticism? Complaining? Are they wide or narrow-minded?

What about their level of self-awareness? Does how they perceive themselves align with a story, or with reality? Do their words align with their actions?

Do they exhibit common sense?

Are they aware of the experience of others? Do they recognize the existence of more than one reality?

How do they relate to others?

How do they handle their own emotions, such as anger, envy, jealousy? How do they handle discomfort? How do they act when things don't go their way?

What about their actions? Do they follow through on what they say they are going to do?

What about grit? What happens when things don't come easy?

Do they take responsibility? Are they accountable?

What about the presence of generosity, kindness?

How has the person behaved in the past?

People are complicated. We all have good days and bad days. We act in ways that leave us feeling like we could have done better.

We are all more than one thing.

This is why I refrain from assuming I can do a quick read on someone's character, and instead observe, listen, and gather answers to the questions above over a period of time.

To Develop Confidence

Create or refine your boundaries. Who are you, and how are you different from "we"? What do you want, and how is that different from what others want for you? What do you really want to do, and who will that disappoint? When do you have trouble saying no, and why?

Now, go disappoint the people who love you. Go learn how to say no.

Get to know the stranger who lives inside of you. Who is she? Which parts of her surprise you? When was the last time she did something unexpected?

Realize how totally cool she is. Learn to love her. She goes first.

This exploration will take the rest of your life.

Create a habit. Do a little bit of something every day. Watch a small thing you do every day become a big thing that defines you.

Set a goal, ideally something almost implausible. Run a marathon. Complete a race. Extra points if in doing this you get super healthy and fit.

Get your shit together. This means different things to different people. In what places are you a mess? Get a filing cabinet. Get your finances in order. Do your laundry. Fold your clothes. Make your bed. Be reliable. Be the person your friends count on.

Step into the fact that you are responsible for yourself and that if you want your life to run, you have to be the one who runs it.

Make a list of things that scare you. I don't mean something that puts you in real danger, like walking down a dark alley in the middle of the night. I mean applying for a job you are not sure you can do. Telling someone how you feel. Facing an awkward situation and navigating its complexities.

Then systematically go through the list and check it off.

Face every single fear you've ever had. Make another list.
Do it again.

Make a list of things you don't think you can do. Rock climbing. Traveling alone. Dancing. Whatever.

Then, systematically go through the list and check it off.

This will often include taking classes, practicing, getting someone to teach you. Go figure it out.

Get your ass kicked. Fail. Don't meet that goal. Fall off the wagon when it comes to that habit you wanted to create. Be rejected from that job you applied to.

Now, get up.

See? You can get up.

Get back on that wagon.

How To Feel Less Overwhelmed

I walk away. I walk away from everything.

I walk across town, look as far as my eyes can see, work through my thoughts not by thinking them but by taking slow, deep breaths.

I do less instead of more.

I procrastinate. Take a nap.

Then, I find a notebook. I ask myself the following questions (and write down the answers):

What is it that I want? What are the things I do that will help me get there? What are all the things I am doing that do not assist in getting me where I want to go?

What makes me feel curious? What makes me feel wonder? What makes me feel alive? Am I doing enough of these things?

I don't ever have all the answers all at once, but I return to this notebook every day. I think a bit each day. Write a bit each day. Do a little bit against what I write, every day.

I accept I will not do everything. I will certainly not do everything all at once.

Just a little bit.

One day not too far from today I will look back and feel awe at all the things I've somehow done.

I will look around and feel stunned at this beautiful place I have arrived at, and the fact that I am here at all will feel a lot like magic.

Good Questions To Ask a Date

What do you like most about yourself?

What are three qualities you appreciate in others?

What do you like least about yourself?

What do you want?

Can you share with me three boundaries that are important to you?

How would you define success?

Describe your perfect day.

Describe your perfect meal.

What do you do when you have nothing to do?

List 10 things you are grateful for.

If you could be really talented at anything, what would that be?

If you could speak any language, which would you choose?

If you could pick up a skill, what would it be?

How old is your oldest friendship?

Name the three people in the world that are most important to you, and tell me about them.

Why did your last relationship end?

Are you on good terms with your exes?

Who do you go to for advice?

Did your parents hug you?

Tell me something you've never told anyone — not a secret, but rather a story you have overlooked.

What are the three most interesting things you have learned about yourself?

What would you like to know about me?

What Will People Think if You Are Always Happy?

My life gets better every time I replace the question "what will people think of me?" with:

Is this good or bad for me?

Is this an expression of who I am?

Is this a boundary I need or want?

How does this make me feel?

How will it make me feel in the future?

Does it align with who I want to be?

And, my favorite:

What will I think of me?

Managing a Difficult Day

First, I attempt to decode what it is I need. A real breakfast. Time out. Time alone. Then I go figure out how I can provide these things to me.

How am I making this harder than it needs to be? Do I need to hold my breath? Do I need to clench my jaw? Do I need my shoulders to be scrunched up?

How can I make this easier? I tend to hold back tears but crying is often truly helpful. Or maybe I can go for a walk. Sit in the sun. Talk to a friend. Possibly all these things at the same time.

What do I need to let go of? (Not to ruin your own exploration but for me the most frequent answer to this question is "my ego.")

I remind myself this is not forever. Every painful feeling feels like this is the way life is going to be now, but bad days move along, eventually becoming distant memories.

Finally, I (somewhat grudgingly) ask myself what this is here to teach me. This makes me feel like at the very least I can turn this into something useful.

The answer to this last question is almost always "patience."

How Do You Know if You're With the 'Right' Person?

If something wonderful or something terrible happens, who is the first person I think of calling?

If I set thoughts aside and get into my body, how do I feel? Tense, strained, tight? Animated, happy? My body is more reliable than my thoughts, because my thoughts have many voices (such as anxiety). When I am with this person, do I experience a sense of ease, well-being?

Do I feel like everything seems fair, harmonious, balanced, the opposite of one-sided? This balance should be clearly reflected everywhere — conversations, finances, chores, planning, decision-making.

Is there fundamental compatibility? Do we complement each other, even in our differences? Do we share similar values?

Am I learning from this person? Do I in many ways feel like this person is making me better? Do I like me when I am with them?

Are they solid? Are they honest, kind? Do they follow through on what they say they are going to do? Is there a sense of commitment?

Do I trust them?

Do we listen?

Do we respect each other?

Do I feel safe enough to feel like I don't need to pretend, or keep my opinions to myself? Do I tell them how I really feel? Are we open with each other, vulnerable?

Do we fight well, not to win, but to protect "us"? To understand each other better? Are we interested in working on our relationship?

Do I like their friends? Do my friends like him?

Do I like him? Setting aside the love, are we friends?

Am I comfortable spending time away from him?

It's normal to experience doubt, ambivalence, boredom, even attraction to other people. It's normal, because we are human and everything inside of us fluctuates.

It's the answers to these questions that tell me what I need to know.

People Always Say "Try New Things". Like What?

In the morning, do you drink coffee? Try tea. Do you eat breakfast early? Eat breakfast late.

Does your inner voice criticize you relentlessly? Find the one who supports you and turn her volume up. Switching the inner voice I listen to counts as "something new".

Does it feel like you have the same fight over and over? Resolve to stop fighting about that particular thing. Resolve — instead of combat — counts as "something new".

Do you have a habit that you wish you could break? Replace it with a new habit that you want. Switching instead of feeling stuck counts as "something new".

Do you hang out with people who leave you wondering why you hang out with them? Begin right away to hang out with those people you wish you had time to see more. Good company counts as "something new".

Do you follow social media accounts that leave you feeling bad about yourself? Find the ones that make you feel inspired. Inspired counts as "something new".

Do you wish you could quit your job? I know. it's hard. But just because it's hard doesn't mean you can't plan. Planning is different than enduring. Planning is "something new".

Do you carry a grudge, or a worry, or a regret? Leave it right outside your door so that it can't come into the space where you live. You can pick it up again on your way out. Taking a break instead of holding it tight is "something new".

Do you keep tension in your body? Release anything — your shoulders, your fingers, your jaw. Relaxing instead of clenching counts as "something new".

Do you feel tired all the time? Instead of more caffeine, catch up on your sleep. Recovery counts as "something new".

So does making things easier on yourself rather than harder. Instead of berating, forgive yourself. Forgive yourself in the name of something new.

How Do I Know if I Have Control Issues?

Do you feel you're always right?

Like your way is the only way?

Like you have to do it or it doesn't get done right?

That when you fight or disagree it's his fault?

Like, he would be perfect if only you could just change, improve, fix him?

I mean, you're only trying to help.

Do you often correct him? Who would wear those shoes with those socks, anyway?

Do you question his choices?

You did what?

Do you give him the silent treatment or shower him with affection depending on how he behaved? What about sex? Is it a reward?

Do you feel like, ugh, he spends too much time alone, too much time with his friends, too much time at work? Do you feel like it's just wrong that he gets along with his ex?

Do you snoop not because you are spying, exactly, but just confirming he is where he said he'd be? Are you, you know, just checking?

When you fight, do you tell him he's — meh. Frankly, not very smart.

Look. I would not have done it that way.

And, shouldn't he just know why you're angry?

Do you tell him he would do what you are asking him to do if he really loved you?

Do you tell him that if he does that one more time, you've had it, you're through?

The Important Questions

Who am I?

What do I want?

What is important to me?

Do I feel a sense of purpose, and if not how can I create it?

Am I a priority to me?

Are the places I am spending my time mapping back to my priorities?

Are my decisions and my values aligned?

How am I measuring my worth?

Am I clearly communicating what I need?

What am I responsible for?

What am I not responsible for?

What are my patterns?

What do I need to recover from?

Where am I pretending?

363

What am I hiding?

What do I need to let go of?

Do I have too much stuff?

What role does fear play in my life?

What role do mistakes play in my life?

What is the effect my relationships have on me?

Where are the places where my boundaries need adjusting?

What am I struggling with, and how can I struggle less, suffer less?

Is This Emotional Cheating?

Am I attempting to lie to myself (or to anyone)?

How much effort am I expending defending, justifying, explaining, rationalizing, apologizing?

Am I being deceptive, lying, hiding, omitting, misleading?

Am I plotting to spend more time with them when I don't really need to?

What am I feeling? Is it turbulent, agitated, disturbed? Where do my thoughts go? Where is my attention?

Is the energy I am putting into this relationship having an impact — affecting, subtracting — energy from my primary relationship?

Is this relationship I am so intent on considering innocuous in any way making up for something I want and am not getting from my main relationship?

Am I creating an allegiance with this person against my main relationship? Am I complaining about my significant other, pointing out flaws and shortcomings?

Why do I need quotation marks when I refer to all this as "harmless"?

Upset

When I am upset I feel my emotions take over. This feels like agitation, distress, internal chaos.

From this place it's so very difficult to do anything other than be upset but I will tell you what I try to remind myself: I am not my emotions.

"I am upset" is not the same as "I feel upset", and this makes all the difference. Because, I can create a degree of separation between who I am and what I feel, positioning myself as a witness, a witness who can see without being tangled up in it.

"Oh, look. I'm feeling upset. Why? What brought this on? What exactly caused it?"

And then *"What story am I telling myself that may or may not be true that has landed my feelings in this overturned place?"*

Behind every episode of distress there is a story. There is always a story. It usually sounds like *"I don't matter! I am not being considered! I am not being heard! Nobody understands me!"*

Finding it is important because it shows me that my feelings relate a lot more to the story that I am telling myself than to the source of my disquiet.

And then *"What do I need? How can I first identify, then find what I need to soothe myself, to take myself from upset to not? How can I take care of myself?"*

I have the ability to get me what I need. (For example, if I don't feel understood, do I understand myself? This is something I can work on.)

It's exercising this ability that can pull me out of my upset, so we (my emotions and I) can slip into something more comfortable.

I AM UPSET!!!

I AM POWERLESS
TO DO ANYTHING
ABOUT IT.

VS

I FEEL UPSET.

I HAVE POWER
TO LOOK AT IT
AND TAKE ACTION.

Am I Emotionally Avoidant?

Do you feel like relationships are not that important?

Do other people frequently seem too needy, too clingy, too much?

Do others frequently overwhelm you?

Do you feel someone is being dramatic when they are trying to tell you how they feel?

Do you have a sense that you are a nuisance and as such try to avoid "bothering" others?

When problems arise in a relationship do you automatically assume there is something wrong with you?

Do you alternate closeness with pushing someone away?

Do you typically stonewall someone during a fight by refusing to react, respond or engage?

Do you resist intimacy?

Are your personal boundaries hard, immutable?

Are you very independent, with a tendency to make your own decisions without talking them over with anyone?

How To Learn From Mistakes

First, compassion. If I would never berate a friend for a mistake, if instead I would be supportive, gentle, encouraging, I extend myself the same courtesy.

I banish blame. Pointing the finger at someone else means less responsibility, and less responsibility means less power.

Instead of bemoaning the mistake, I ask *"what is this here to teach me?"* (Sometimes I need to bemoan for a few days before asking this question so I also try to give myself time to hurt if that's what I need to do.)

I write down — or draw — the series of events that led to the mistake to find the place where things could have gone differently. I find this particularly useful when I make the same mistake over and over: to alter a pattern, first I have to find it.

Talking about patterns, I ask why. Why does this happen, or keep happening? What is this tied to? (Spoiler: if I make a mistake, it's usually my ego trying to re-establish her dominion.)

When I find the pattern, I ask myself what is the mini, tiny, small, incremental step I can take to carve a new pattern. I find small steps more effective than any grand plans I make and then abandon.

I recruit every resource available to me. This might be a book, a friend I can talk to, a class I can take. It might be a time out.

I look back. Sometimes when I feel I never learn, when I am convinced I am stuck and unable to make progress, I look back to see how far I've come.

Propinquity

I use my phone so much that it's fair to say that how I use my phone is how I live my life. If I want to live better, I have to be deliberate about how I use it.

Have you heard of the Propinquity Effect? It states that what is physically closest to me has the biggest effect on how I experience the world.

My phone is not a phone. It's a conduit between me and everything. It has a direct impact not just on what I do, but on how I perceive.

Being idle invites my brain to think new thoughts. I crowd out every idle instant by checking a device that I don't need to check, since I just did, a second ago.

These are the questions I ask myself:

Do I check my phone when I don't need to?

Is the time I spend on it switching my brain on (learning something new, opening up to a new perspective) or off (mindless scrolling)?

Is what I am seeing making me feel good (inspired, connected) or bad (like I'm missing out, like my life is not good enough, like I need to buy, buy)?

371

Is my phone keeping me from my feelings? What is it? Am I lonely, bored, anxious? Am I using my phone to avoid having a moment with my own thoughts? This is where creativity comes from, connection, self-awareness. Being alone with my phone is not the same as being with me.

Is my phone affecting real social interaction? Am I looking at my phone instead of at you? Am I making the people I love feel like they don't matter?

The secret to happiness is being here. Am I ever here? If not, I will be anxious and frazzled and unmoored. I will feel uneasy and dissatisfied and wonder what the meaning of life is, since I'm always somewhere else, and the meaning of life is here.

When Life Has Become Monotonous

If you are bored or feel like your life has become monotonous:

Think. Observe your thoughts. Where do they go? What do they think? A bored brain is in a good place to solve problems, make things better, get inspired, incite change.

Clean something. Clean a drawer, your home, your computer, your room. As you get into cleaning, donate anything you don't really use. Sorting your outsides sorts your insides. Make room for something new.

Make a list of things you are interested in. Plan to pursue them. This can look like reading a book, watching some videos, taking a class, or taking a trip. It can be a pursuit to fill an hour or to change the course of your life.

Learn something new. Learn something improbable. Learn something you never thought you could be good at. Afraid of public speaking? Take an improv class. Afraid of heights? Learn how to rock climb. Learn something that will show you you can do something you didn't think you could.

Dream big, then start small. What do you dream of, in that world of unlikely things? Writing a book? Spending a year somewhere else? How can you break this big dream into small steps? Take a step to inch you closer to your dream every day.

Exercise. Go for a walk, a stroll, a run, a swim. Take a yoga class. Exercise helps your brain get unstuck.

Make something. It can be anything — a cake, a dish, a cookie, a drawing, a collage, a sweater.

Reconnect with nature. Find a park, a beach, a hiking trail, a forest. Take deep breaths of fresh air. Stretch. Bring nature inside by keeping plants at home. Learn how to take care of them — it's a skill you can learn.

Observe what you complain about, in particular if you complain about it over and over. Go fix it.

Make yourself happy. What makes you happy? Friends? Painting? Talking? Watching a movie? A bath? Give yourself the gift of whatever makes you feel joy, pleasure.

Do something that sets you up for a better future. Have that difficult conversation you have been putting off. Set a boundary with someone who makes you feel taken advantage of. Turn something you do every day (such as getting up in the morning) into a ritual. This will eventually shift "I feel bored" to "I feel at peace."

I'M BORED.

NO YOU'RE NOT:

OBSERVE YOUR OWN THOUGHTS.

CLEAN SOMETHING.

MAKE A LIST.

LEARN SOMETHING NEW.

DREAM BIG. START SMALL.

EXERCISE.

MAKE SOMETHING.

RECONNECT WITH NATURE.

FIX IT.

MAKE YOURSELF HAPPY.

SET UP YOUR OWN BETTER FUTURE.

DZDR

375

I Feel Bad About Myself.
How Do I Improve?

Pull out a piece of lined paper.

Scrawl in large letters at the top: *Look forward, not back.*

Make a list of things that would make you feel proud of yourself. Encouraged. That would make you regard yourself with respect.

Then, sit back and look at your list.

What would it take, to accomplish the things you have written?

Break each thing down into small steps.

For example: would completing a marathon be satisfying? Then a small step is to talk to a trainer who can give you advice beyond *"run every day".*

Then, make another list of actions that best represent you. If you acted out of character, what would be in character?

Then sit back and look at this second list.

What would it take, to be this person full of character?

Break each thing down into small steps.

For example: be more patient with the people that I love. A day at a time. If one day I get impatient, I just get back on the wagon.

You can dwell on the past all you want, beat yourself up and live tormented by the things you have done or failed to do.

You can let disappointment and guilt swallow you whole.

Or you can accept you can't change these things, and focus on changing what you can.

If you screw up one day, you get to start over the next day.

Dealing With Jealousy or Envy

What is it that is good in me?

What is good in my life? Do I see it?

Do I value the right things?

Do I have a sense of purpose, and if not, how can I create it?

Do I feel safe, and if I don't, how can I give that to myself?

Am I aware of my expectations and assumptions? Where do they come from? Do they contribute to my growth, or my suffering?

When I feel like I want what others have, what is it that I am really lacking inside myself, and how can I get it?

What things do I do that feed jealousy and envy? Egocentricity? Gossip? Comparison? Malice? Revenge? Contempt? Competition? How can I move my focus away from these?

What am I afraid of?

Are the people I surround myself with grateful, or people who cannot seem to ever have enough?

How can I get better at celebrating the success of others?

Crisis or Adventure?

What do you do right when you wake up in the morning? Do you seize the day, or does the day ambush you?

Your inner voice — the one you hold a running conversation with. Friend or foe?

Take a look at the people you spend the most time with. Do you like them? Are they allies?

What about pleasure? How often is he a companion? Do you stop to take in the smell of your coffee, savor your breakfast, put on soft socks, kiss someone longer than what is practical or wise?

Do you pause often and fully occupy this pause? You can steal a pause from almost any moment. Do you?

How packed is your day? Is it so busy you are mostly on automatic? And, when you are not busy, do you fill your time? How? What do you read, watch? Does it turn your brain on, or off?

How programmed is your life? Is there room for serendipity?

How do you make your decisions? Do you trust yourself? Are you someone you can count on?

Are you learning new things? How often do you feel wonder? Gratitude? Disbelief?

What are you creating?

Who do you love? How much? With caution or abandon?

Do you know how to say no? Do you say yes a lot?

Do you equate uncertainty with a crisis or with adventure?

wow!

DZDI

383

Author's note:

Thank you for reading my book!

If you have questions about anything along the way, I suggest you enter my name and any key word — self-love, boundaries, ego, relationships — in the Quora search window. This way you can find everything I've written about what you seek, and maybe come across other helpful things along the way.

You can also post comments and questions on Instagram, using the hashtag #dushkazapatachecklistshebang.

Also, other books I've written expand on what I write about here. I particularly recommend my book about boundaries *"How To Draw Your Boundaries and why no one else can help you"*, my workbook about learning how to love yourself *"The Love of Your Life is You: A Step-by-Step Workbook to Loving Yourself"* and a book that explores some of the same themes in a bit more detail *"Feelings Are Fickle and other things I wish someone had told me"*.

Remember that everything I write — including all of the content of the books I mention above — is available on Quora for free.

If you find any of this helpful, please write Amazon reviews so that other people who need it can find it too.

Dushka Zapata

San Francisco, California

May 2022

About the Illustrator

Dan Roam is the author of six international bestselling books on visual storytelling. **The Back of the Napkin** was named by Fast Company, The London Times, and BusinessWeek as the "Creativity Book of the Year".

Dan is a creative director, author, painter, and model-builder. His purpose in life is to make complex things clear by drawing them and to help others do the same. Dan has helped leaders at Allbirds, Google, Microsoft, Boeing, Gap, IBM, the US Navy, and the Obama White House solve complex problems with simple pictures.

Dan and his whiteboard have appeared on CNN, MSNBC, ABC, CBS, Fox, and NPR.

About the Author

Dushka Zapata has worked in communications for over twenty years, running agencies (such as Edelman and Ogilvy) and working with companies to develop their corporate strategy.

During this time she specialized in executive equity and media and presentation training. She helped people communicate better through key message refinement and consistency and coached them to smoothly manage difficult interviews with press during times of crisis.

Dushka is an executive coach and public speaker who imparts workshops about personal brand development. She has been hired for strategic alignment hiring, to coach and mentor high potential individuals, improve upon new business pitches, refine existing processes and galvanize a company's communication efforts.

She recently built and ran the communications team at Zendesk and is now head of communications for Forte, a start up that believes games can unlock new economic opportunities for billions of people.

Dushka is the author of twelve books: "How to be Ferociously Happy", "Amateur: an inexpert, inexperienced, unauthoritative, enamored view of life", "A Spectacular Catastrophe and other things I recommend", "Your Seat Cushion is a Flotation Device and other buoyant short stories", "Someone Destroyed My Rocket Ship and other havoc I have witnessed at the office", "How to Build a Pillow Fort and other valuable life lessons", "You Belong Everywhere and other things you'll have to see for yourself", "Love Yourself and other insurgent acts that recast everything", "Feelings Are Fickle and other things I wish someone had told me", "How to Draw Your Boundaries and why no one else can save you", "The Love of Your Life Is You: A Step-By-Step Workbook to Loving Yourself", and the one you have in your hands.

Dushka was named one of the top 25 innovators in her industry by The Holmes Report and regularly contributes to Quora, the question and answer site, where she has over 190 million views.

Made in the USA
Las Vegas, NV
25 April 2023

71053681R00236